A Century of
CROSS-CHANNEL
PASSENGER FERRIES

Previous page: A swirl of activity as the LBSCR steamer *Sussex* arrives in Dieppe sometime around the turn of the century. The flag signals on her yard indicate the number of passengers on board, first class to port and second and third classes to starboard. The same company's paddle steamer *Paris* is alongside. *Author's Collection*

Below: The end of an era. Dressed to mark the occasion Sealink's last traditional turbine passenger steamer *Caesarea* leaving Folkestone on 4th October 1980 for her final Channel crossing to Boulogne. *Author*

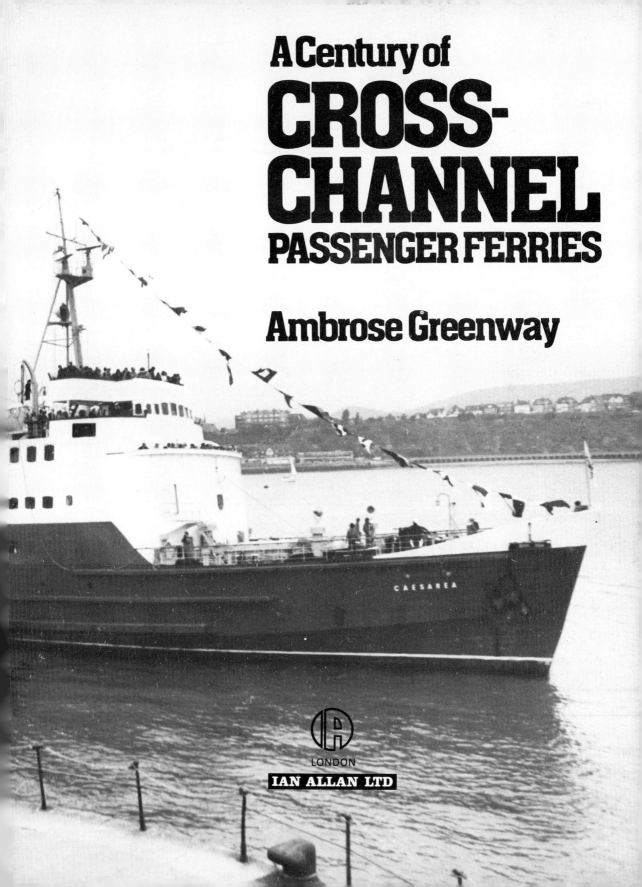

A Century of
CROSS-CHANNEL
PASSENGER FERRIES

PASSENGER FERRIES

Ambrose Greenway

CAESAREA

LONDON
IAN ALLAN LTD

First published 1981

ISBN 0 7110 1069 2

© Ambrose Greenway, 1981

Published by Ian Allan Ltd, Shepperton, Surrey,
and printed by Ian Allan Printing Ltd at their works
at Coombelands in Runnymede, England.

Front cover, top: French paddle steamer *Le Nord* built for the
Nord Rly Co in 1898. *Author's Collection*

Front cover, centre: One of the Belgian *Prinses Astrid*
quartette of 1930 breasts a head sea whilst approaching
Dover. *A.M.S. Russell Collection*

Front cover, bottom: British Rail's *Caesarea* of 1960 seen off
Portland was withdrawn in October 1980 bringing to a close
the era of the traditional British cross-Channel passenger
steamer. *Author*

Back cover, top: South Eastern Rly paddle steamer *Louise
Dagmar* of 1880 leaving Boulogne for her dash to
Folkestone. *Author's Collection*

Back cover, bottom: Belgian Marine's fine motorship *Prinses
Paola* of 1966 seen leaving Dover during her first year of
operation is the last traditional cross-Channel passenger
ship to be built. *Author*

Contents

The line drawings reproduced on the pages
shown were taken from the following
publications:

The Engineer pp43 (*Riviera*), 60 (*Rouen,
Paris*)

Engineering pp63 (*Seaford*), 72 (*Tamise*)

Shipbuilding and Shipping Record pp48
(*Canterbury*), 103 (*Isle of Jersey*), 117 (*St
Patrick*)

The Shipbuilder and Marine Engine Builder
p71 (*Brighton*)

Introduction

My father communicated his love of the sea and ships to me whilst I was still at an early age and it was at Newhaven during occasional forays from our Sussex home that I first experienced the excitement of watching the Channel steamers slip out of harbour on their 64-mile dash to Dieppe.

I particularly recall another visit to Folkestone in 1951 when we had gone for a walk on the Leas before lunch to enjoy the magnificent view of the Channel. A fast and as yet unidentified steamer was approaching head on from the direction of the distant cliffs of Cap Blanc Nez. I watched rivetted as she neared the harbour and swung gracefully to starboard to reveal herself as the sleek new French steamer *Cote d'Azur*. Her profile shortened again as she turned, pausing only momentarily before gathering way astern for her final approach to the breakwater. I followed her until she was alongside and from that moment on I was well and truly hooked.

The love affair born on those Folkestone heights has continued unabated to the present day and it is my hope in writing this book that I shall be able to pass on and share some of my feelings with others.

I freely admit from the outset that Channel passenger steamers are a far from neglected subject and there already exist a number of excellent books about them. However it is now 40 years since Grasemann & McLachlan produced their *English Channel Packet Boats* and as much has happened since then I make no excuse for returning to the subject once again.

Today a new generation is growing up to whom the traditional cross-Channel passenger steamer is almost as remote as a steam engine. Their's is the world of the large multi-purpose car ferry and if they come to read this I hope that they may learn to appreciate something of the grace of the smaller ships which paved the way to today's comparative giants. As for the older generation who have seen it all before I ask them to bear with me in my indulgence and perhaps take a gentle trip down memory lane.

As I write this early in 1980 only three pure passenger ships remain in operation on the Channel and then only regularly during the summer months. Hovercraft and more recently jetfoils are pointing the way to the future and their advent makes it extremely unlikely that any more traditional ships will ever be built. Their story therefore is almost complete.

The 'hundred years' that I have chosen to cover extends to the present day but it is by no means arbitrary and I have bent it slightly in one or two instances to suit my purpose. My reasons for choosing such a period are twofold, first because it conveniently spans the evolution of the 'modern' cross-Channel passenger ship from the days of the original steel built paddle steamers which had finally shaken free from the last clipper-bowed vestiges of the sailing ship era. Secondly photographs of ships built before 1880 are hard to come by and as this is intended to be a more visual record than hitherto I feel that I can omit them with a clear conscience.

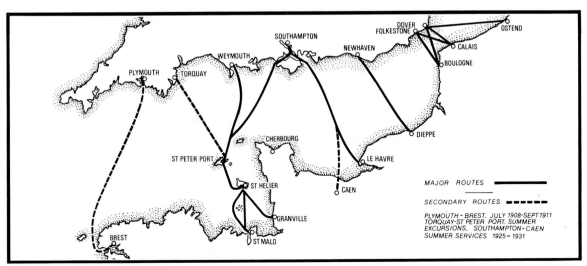

MAJOR ROUTES
SECONDARY ROUTES
PLYMOUTH - BREST. JULY 1908-SEPT 1911
TORQUAY-ST PETER PORT. SUMMER
EXCURSIONS. SOUTHAMPTON - CAEN
SUMMER SERVICES 1925-1931

I have dealt with each ship or groups of similar ships in chronological order in the areas in which they operated, starting in the East Channel with the Dover-Ostend service and proceeding westwards to Weymouth. The French-built steamers are grouped separately in both the Dover and Newhaven sections, even though the ships on the latter service were jointly owned. I have done this to give the reader a clearer picture of the different line of development followed by the French naval architects.

For reasons of space I have confined myself to those ships specifically built for *regular* English Channel service which will explain my apparent omission of the French ALA ships and Dutch Zealand line ships which used Folkestone for a while, also the one or two smaller GWR Irish Sea ships which filled in occasionally on the Weymouth service.

I have received a great deal of help from many quarters in the course of my research and I would like to record my gratitude first and foremost to my good friends Laurence and Jennifer Dunn who have guided and succoured me in my task with unfailing patience. I must also thank the following friends each of whom has contributed from his own fund of knowledge; Mr Peter Bailey of the Newhaven and Seaford Historical Society;

Colonel Robert Gabriel of Bournemouth; Mr David Lyon of the National Maritime Museum; Mr Richard Pryde of Lloyd's Register of Shipping who has dealt with my many queries with admirable cheerfulness; Mr Arthur Russell of Lymington; and lastly but by no means least M. Rene Tetreau of Chatou, France. To the many others too numerous to mention who have helped with information or photographs I record my collective thanks.

Finally if my efforts in producing this book bring to others just a little of the enjoyment that I have gained through my interest in cross-Channel steamers over the years, then I will rest satisfied.

London   *Ambrose Greenway*
January 1980

Photographic Note
Whilst I have made every effort to verify the sources of photographs taken from my own collection there are inevitably one or two instances on the fringe of the statutory 50 year period where I have been unsuccessful and if I have inadvertently infringed anyone's copyright I apologise wholeheartedly.

Abbreviations

Bhp	Brake horsepower		**SE**	Single ended
DE	Double ended		**SECR**	South Eastern & Chatham Railway
F&RR	Fishguard & Rosslare Railways & Harbours		**SER**	South Eastern Railway
GWR	Great Western Railway		**Shp**	Shaft horsepower
HP	High pressure		**SR**	Southern Railway
ihp	Indicated horsepower		**w/t**	Water tube
LBSCR	London, Brighton & South Coast Railway			
LCDR	London, Chatham & Dover Railway		**Note**	
LP	Low pressure		Length = Length between perpendiculars unless otherwise stated	
LSWR	London & South Western Railway			
nhp	Nominal horsepower		Breadth = Moulded breadth	
oa	Overall		Depth = Depth to upper deck (occasionally to a	
r/t	Return tube		higher deck)	

Funnel Colours

Belgium

Belgian Marine	deep buff until 1930 when black top added; from 1973 pale yellow with narrow black top and light blue RTM monogram outlined in dark blue

France

Nord & Ouest Rly Cos	white with black top
SAGA	white with black top
SNCF	buff with black top until 1965 when changed to red with black top, white SNCF monogram added 1973.

UK

LCDR	white with narrow black top
SER	white with deep black top
SECR	white with black top
GWR, F&RR	red with black top
SR, BTC (Southern Region)	buff with black top
BRB from 1965	red with black top and white BR linked rails monogram (Newhaven-Dieppe joint service ships retained their buff funnels to which was later added the joint service flag though this did not apply to the remaining passenger ships

PART 1

Dover to Ostend

Belgian Marine Administration

Prins Albert, Ville de Douvres, La Flandre

At the start of the 1880s the Belgian Government's Ostend to Dover mail service was being operated by seven clipper-bowed paddle steamers which had come from the Hoboken yard of the Societe Anonyme John Cockerill between 1867 and 1873. Upon reorganisation of the service in 1882, which brought about a reduction in fares, these steamers maintained a twice daily service taking about five hours.

With increased demand calling for three services a day a pair of larger steamers were ordered from Cockerill's in 1886. The first of these, *Prins Albert* made her maiden crossing on 1 April 1887 followed by the *Ville de Douvres* on 13 May. Neither ship came up to expectation and the former was quickly returned to the builders where she was re-engined and re-boilered, the opportunity also being taken to increase her length by 15ft. On reappearing in her new guise on 23 September 1889 she reached a speed of 19kts, a similar speed being obtained by her sister who, altered in like manner, re-entered service on 16 February 1890 some two and a half months after the third sister *La Flandre* whose design incorporated the improvements from scratch.

The three ships shared the following main particulars:

Length: 271ft 8in
Breadth: 29ft 0in
Depth/Draught: 15ft 6in/9ft 7in
Gross tonnage: 860
Machinery: Compound diagonal
(*Prins Albert* originally simple oscillating)
Boilers: Four single ended 120lb/sq in
Power: 4,300ihp
Speed: 17kts (designed)

Two-deck ships with a raised turtle back foc's'le they had two raking closely spaced funnels whose horizontal tops introduced a style that was to be a feature of Belgian built Channel steamers until the advent of *Prinses Astrid* in 1930.

To maintain the new thrice-daily service in 1888 whilst its own ships were rebuilding, the Belgian Government were forced to charter in the Blohm & Voss paddler *Freia* and the Barrow owned *Manx Queen* (ex-*Duchess of Edinburgh*). However once their own ships had finally entered service they continued to perform satisfactorily for about 20 years.

Prins Albert was taken out of service in 1908 and three years later was sold to Forth Shipbreakers for scrapping. *Ville de Douvres* was sold in the same year to Turkey but the third sister, *La Flandre*, survived until 1918 when the retreating German army sank her as a blockship in Ostend harbour.

Below: An early photograph of *Ville de Douvres* at sea. Prior to her rebuild she had looked much more primitive with tall, bell-mouth funnels. *Author's Collection*

Princesse Henriette, Princesse Josephine

Towards the end of 1887 the Scottish shipbuilders William Denny & Co of Dumbarton were successful in obtaining an important order from the Belgian Government for a fast new mail steamer of over 1,000ton gross. Though the conditions were most stringent, stipulating the high speed of 20.5kts on a length not exceeding 300ft, Denny's, thanks to their new testing tank and a new type of lighter, more powerful machinery, were able to deliver the *Princesse Henriette* within the required seven months. They thus began a reputation for building fine cross-Channel steamers that was to last about 70 years.

A sister ship had been ordered while the other ship was building and, named *Princesse Josephine* at her launch on 14 August 1888, was delivered some three months later. The main dimensions of the pair were as follows:

Length: 300ft 0in
Breadth: 38ft 0in
Depth/Draught: 13ft 6in/8ft 8in
Gross tonnage: 1,101/1,119
Machinery: Compound diagonal
Boilers: Six Admiralty 110lb/sq in
Power: 7,000ihp max
Speed: 20.5kts

Unique in the Belgian fleet through being double-enders (this was due to restrictions in Ostend) they were also

fitted with bow rudders. Their two widely spaced raking funnels gave them a slightly unbalanced profile, but internally their accommodation was of a luxury nature, berths being provided for 80 first class passengers.

Having obtained 21.09kts on the Clyde, *Princesse Henriette* covered the distance between Dover and Ostend on her initial trip in 2hr 55min, and between them the two ships enabled the scheduled time to be reduced to 3hr 20min. Both had long careers marred only by the unfortunate collision between *Princesse Henriette* and *Comtesse de Flandre* in fog on 29 March 1889 which resulted in the loss of the latter along with 11 lives.

Above: A striking view of *Princesse Henriette* in wartime dazzle paint. Note the wide spacing of her funnels. *IWM*

The *Princesse Josephine* was out of commission when the Germans invaded Belgium in 1914 and she was seized, being eventually sunk as a blockship at Bruges in 1918. Her sister ship helped to carry most of the National Bank's gold reserves to England before serving as a troopship for the duration of the war. After a brief return to peacetime service she was withdrawn in 1920 and was scrapped in Holland the following year.

Leopold II

At the end of 1891 the Belgian Government expressed a desire to order two new mailboats and following protracted negotiations Denny's were contracted to build one of them, helped no doubt by the success of the previous ships. Although the conditions imposed were as strict as ever, certain latitude in design was permitted which resulted in a ship of very pleasing appearance.

Named *Leopold II* she was delivered in April 1893 having obtained a mean speed of 21.95kts over four runs between Cloch and Cumbrae and 22.16kts on the measured mile. She had the following main particulars:

Length: 340ft 0in
Breadth: 38ft 0in
Depth: 15ft 0in
Gross tonnage: 1,632
Machinery: Compound diagonal surface condensing
Boilers: Eight single ended forced draught
Four forward and four aft of engine room
Power: 8,800ihp
Speed: 21.5kts

Her steel hull was divided into 13 watertight compartments and her extra 40ft in length over the

earlier vessels allowed a normal counter stern and happier spacing of her lofty, raking funnels. Over 400 passengers could be carried in the well-appointed steam-heated accommodation which included 10 staterooms in the deckhouse between the funnels and a special stateroom for the King of Belgium abaft the second funnel.

Trouble with her high pressure cylinder caused her to return to Dumbarton for its replacement after only about six months' operation but she later settled down to cross regularly in 3hr 10min, though she tended to be rather heavy on coal consumption.

Used as a troopship during World War 1 she was sold to the British Shipping Administration in 1920 in exchange for two trawlers and eventually sold for scrapping in Germany in March, 1922. She was the last Belgian Channel ferry to be built in Britain, all subsequent ships coming from the Cockerill yard.

Marie Henriette

The second of the 1891 orders went to John Cockerill whose Hoboken yard, spurred on no doubt to better the Denny-built ship, delivered the impressive *Marie Henriette* in 1893. Her introduction released the 1869 built clipper-bowed ship of that name.

Although she shared the same basic dimensions as *Leopold II* (qv) she nevertheless betrayed her Belgian origin with her flat topped raking funnels giving her a rather stiff but powerful appearance.

Apart from external differences national pride was probably responsible for her machinery being given larger cylinders and longer piston stroke, the latter's 84in ranking amongst the largest ever attained. The resulting increase in power of some 300ihp compared with her

near sister gave her a trial speed of 22.2kts which was claimed as a world record for paddle driven Channel steamers.

She became the holder of a less enviable record when after leaving Dover in a severe storm in January 1902 she lost the use of her starboard paddle wheel and after spending periods drifting out of control and in tow of a Belgian tug she eventually reached Ostend in tow of *La Flandre* after a passage of 64hr; a far cry indeed from her more normal 3hr 10min.

A good sea boat and successful in service she was used for the transport of wounded at the beginning of World War 1 and whilst acting in this capacity stranded on rocks near Cape Barfleur in October 1914 on passage to

Cherbourg. 650 persons were rescued by a destroyer and it later transpired that her loss was due to the lighthouse being out of action — a fact unknown to her master at the time.

Above: The powerful *Marie Henriette* seen at sea. Her stranding early in World War 1 was a sad and premature end to a fine ship. *Author's Collection*

Rapide

This steamer was delivered by Cockerill's to the Belgian Government in 1895. Although built on the same lines as the previous two ships she was quite a bit smaller, being designed in the main for the slower overnight crossing and with this in mind much attention was paid to fuel economy.

Her main particulars were:

Length: 300ft 0in
Breadth: 38ft 0in

Below: The Belgian built *Rapide* had shorter funnels than the *Leopold II* but was very similar to her in other respects. *Author's Collection*

Depth: 13ft 6in
Gross tonnage: 1,195
Machinery: Compound diagonal
Power: 7,000ihp
Speed: 20kts

A steady and reliable ship, *Rapide* made 20.83kts on trials and was unique among the Belgian built paddlers in having sloping funnel tops.

During a storm on 4 December 1896 she was flung against the piles of Dover Admiralty pier but suffered only slight damage. Surviving World War 1 she was sold for scrap in 1923 after a useful if unspectacular life of 28 years.

Princesse Clementine

What was to turn out to be the final Belgian paddler was launched at Hoboken by Crown Prince Albert in October 1896 and entered service in June of the following year. Broadly similar to *Marie Henriette* in size and looks she had the following particulars:

Length: 341ft 3in
Breadth: 37ft 8in
Depth: 14ft 2in
Gross tonnage: 1,474
Machinery: Compound diagonal
Boilers: Eight single-ended Serve type
Power: 9,200ihp
Speed: 22kts

Constructed of mild steel her hull was sub-divided by 12 watertight bulkheads. Three decks including a large bridge deck allowed about 700 passengers to be carried in luxuriously appointed accommodation which included three large royal staterooms, 12 private cabins and a smokeroom in houses on the upper deck. Additionally she was the first of the fleet to be fitted with wireless telegraphy, operating through La Panne.

On her initial trials in poor weather in the Clyde she recorded a speed of 22.18kts with her engines developing 8,500ihp though on a later attempt she raised this to 22.5kts at about 9,300ihp.

Following the outbreak of war she operated for a short while from Folkestone along with her sisters and was later used to carry the Royal Marines to Belgium. Based

*Below: **Princesse Clementine** on trials. The small ventilator on top of her wheelhouse and an extra pair of boats forward distinguished her from the very similar Marie Henriette. Author's Collection*

*Bottom: Comparison between this quarter view of **Princesse Clementine** and that of Leopold II shows up the stiffer appearance of the Belgian-built ships. Author's Collection*

at Cherbourg under the control of the Belgian War Office she was lent to the British Government in May 1915 and spent the remainder of the war years transporting troops to France from Folkestone and Southampton.

After the war she returned to her normal run, proving to be still capable of 22kts, but after the introduction of the new *Princesse Marie-Jose* in 1923 she was placed in reserve at Ostend. Put up for sale by auction in June 1928 she attracted several bids but was sold to French shipbreakers for £6,400. She had worked hard for all but five of her 31 years and (at the time of her demise) was the last surviving example of a cross-Channel paddle steamer.

Princesse Elisabeth

Following the lead given by the South Eastern and Chatham and the London, Brighton and South Coast Railways, the Belgian Government were quick to order a turbine-driven steamer from Cockerill's, but as the latter's engine works at Seraing lacked experience in this field a set of Parsons turbines were ordered from England.

The new ship was larger than the two British examples and named *Princesse Elisabeth* she had the following main particulars:

Length: 357ft 0in
Breadth: 40ft 0in
Depth of hold: 23ft 2in
Gross tonnage: 1,747
Machinery: One HP and two LP turbines

Below: The Belgian Government's first turbine steamer *Princesse Elisabeth* **became the fastest merchant ship in the world when she attained a speed of 24.6kts on trials.** *Author's Collection*

Boilers: Four cylindrical (Babcock & Wilcox w/t after
World War 1)
Power: 12,000shp
Speed: 22.25kts (designed service)

Her design incorporated two closely mounted funnels of
the by now standard Belgian pattern placed well forward
on a long deck house which rested on a low flush hull with
straight stem and well rounded cruiser stern.

During trials in the Scheldt she made 24.8kts but later
she reached 26.25kts in the Clyde which made her the
fastest ship in the world until the advent of the
Mauretania. Her astern speed was 16kts and she was
stopped from 20kts in 2½ times her length in 1.25min.

Hailed as the first turbine steamer to be built on the
Continent she could accommodate 1,100 passengers and
her public rooms lacked none of the ornamentation
found in the later paddlers. She helped to boost the
number of passengers carried on the route by over 18,000
in her first two years of operation.

Before World War 2 her small wheelhouse was raised
a deck and moved aft of the forward mast, cabs being
fitted at the same time to bring her into line with the next
two ships. When war broke out she was lying at Antwerp
with her engines dismantled but she just managed to get
away to England before the Germans arrived,
completing her refit in London.

She was later used as a hospital ship under British
control and was handed back to Belgium on 3 September
1919. During her postwar refit the opportunity was taken
to replace her original boilers with new water tube units
from Babcock & Wilcox. Thus re-equipped she returned
to her normal peacetime service on which she remained
until superseded by new tonnage in 1930 and was sold for
scrap the following year.

Jan Breydel, Pieter de Coninck

Following the success of *Princesse Elisabeth* and in
anticipation of increased passenger traffic for the 1910
Brussels Exhibition two more turbine steamers were
ordered from Hoboken. Closely approximating the
earlier ship in design they were delivered in 1909 and
1910 being given the Flemish names *Jan Breydel* and
Pieter de Coninck respectively. Later ships were named
alternately in French and Flemish.

Both ships shared the following main particulars:

Length (oa): 361ft 0in
Breadth: 40ft 0in
Depth: 23ft 2in
Gross tonnage: 1,750
Machinery: One HP and two LP turbines

Boilers: Eight Scotch forced draught
Power: 13,500shp
Speed: 22kts

On initial trials in the Scheldt they both reached 24.25kts
but *Jan Breydel* later raised this to 24.9kts in the Clyde
on 12 April 1910. The low hull was divided into ten
watertight compartments and the sterns, following
previous practice, were liberally adorned with
'gingerbread'. During the exhibition year the new ships
helped to swell the number of travelling passengers to
nearly a quarter of a million.

With war declared and the invading Germans already
on Belgian soil *Jan Breydel* was used to carry the Queen
of the Belgians and her children to England, returning

Left: *Jan Breydel* at sea showing the 'gingerbread' decoration on her stern. The Belgian ships showed their names on their sterns only until 1930. *Author's Collection*

Below: This 1920s view of *Jan Breydel* backing towards her berth in Dover Harbour shows her with the forward end of her superstructure plated in. The two small ventilators behind her wheelhouse were peculiar to her and her sister. Taller ventilators of equal height were later fitted alongside both funnels. *Author's Collection*

Bottom: *Pieter de Coninck* leaving Dover in 1930 with partly plated in superstructure. Her funnel cowls have been removed and black tops added. Note the single cowl ventilator between second funnel and mainmast which distinguished her from her sister. *Author's Collection*

her alone to Antwerp on 7 September. On 6 October the same ship carried most of the Belgian diplomatic corps to Le Havre. Both ships were subsequently lent to the Admiralty to satisfy the urgent need for hospital ships.

During their ten years of postwar service both ships had the forward ends of their promenade decks plated-in and after 1930 their funnel tops were painted black.

In 1931 *Pieter de Coninck* was sold for scrap but *Jan Breydel* was sold to an owner in the Middle East who proposed a North African coastal service. Renamed *Tourist* she underwent a million franc conversion but her new owner defaulted and she was seized by creditors. She lay in Antwerp for a further two years before being sold to a Ghent shipbreaker.

Stad Antwerpen, Ville de Liege

Following the sale of their two paddle steamers in 1911 leaving a fleet of seven paddlers and three turbines, the Belgian authorities decided to order a further pair of turbine ships. They were originally intended to be the fastest yet but economic sense prevailed and they were designed as smaller, slower units to operate the less well patronised winter schedules, carrying 900 passengers.

Delivered from Hoboken in 1913 and early 1914 the *Stad Antwerpen* and *Ville de Liege* had the following dimensions:

Length: 300ft 0in
Breadth: 36ft 0in
Depth of hold: 22ft 9in
Gross tonnage: 1,384
Machinery: Three sets Cockerill turbines
(One HP, two LP) direct drive
Boilers: Eight Babcock & Wilcox w/t forced draught
Power: 12,000shp
Speed: 23.5kts

Being about 50ft shorter than the previous ships but retaining the same closely spaced funnels, these ships had an altogether more compact profile. Their fuller sterns however made them difficult to steer when going astern and their extra top hamper gave them a tendency to roll. To counter this Frahm anti-rolling tanks were tried in both ships but the extra weight of water (30ton) gave rise to fears of further loss of stability and they were removed.

During World War 1 *Ville de Liege* was used as a hospital ship for the Belgian army at Calais and later both were taken over by the Admiralty for trooping and hospital duties. After the war they brought the first Belgian exiles back to Ostend in January 1919.

Below: *Stad Antwerpen* and her sister were shorter and more compact than the earlier Belgian ships and their mainmasts were mounted on a prominent deckhouse. Note the old motor car on her stern. *Author's Collection*

Above: A 1930s view of *Stad Antwerpen*
**showing alterations to her superstructure
and funnels.** *Author's Collection*

Below: A profile of *Ville de Liege* **following
her conversion to the side-loading car
ferry** *London-Istanbul* **showing her four
ramps. She was a pioneer in the use of the
roll-on, roll-off principle.**

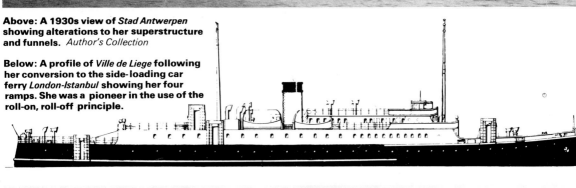

In October 1934 *Stad Antwerpen* was sold at public auction to Belgian breakers but in February 1936 her sister, whose hull was in better condition following repairs made after grounding on rocks outside Dover Harbour in February 1929, was taken in hand for conversion to a car ferry. Her hull was gutted and two boilers and one funnel were removed, the remaining four boilers being regrouped and converted to oil burning. She was fitted with four starboard mounted boarding ramps of different heights to cope with tidal range and her capacity was 100 cars, whilst passenger capacity and speed were reduced to 200 and 21.5kts respectively.

Renamed *London Istanbul* she re-entered service in August with two vertical masts and a short upright funnel

Above: A port side view of *London-Istanbul* **leaving Dover. In
1941 she was converted to a minesweeper depot ship by
Barclay Curle and commissioned as HMS** *Ambitious* **early in
1942 for service at Scapa Flow.** *Author's Collection*

to bring her profile more into line with the new motor ships. She ran successfully until World War 2, from which she emerged unscathed, reopening the mail service in 1946. She was eventually withdrawn after the introduction of a new purpose-built car ferry in 1949 and laid up in Ostend. British Rail chartered her for Dover/Folkestone-Calais operation but she was found to be unserviceable and went for scrap in October of the following year.

Princesse Marie-Jose

The only new Belgian steamer to be built in the 1920s was the *Princesse Marie-Jose*. Launched at Hoboken by Cockerills on 19 October 1922, she entered service the following year, and was the first Belgian Channel ship to employ geared turbines and twin screws, some 11 years after this form of propulsion was first used by the LSWR. Her main particulars were as follows:

Length: 348ft 0in
Breadth: 40ft 0in
Depth of hold: 23ft 9in
Gross tonnage: 1,767
Machinery: Two sets Parsons/Cockerill
single reduction geared turbines
Boilers: Eight
Power: 13,500shp
Speed: 23kts

Closely resembling the 1910-built pair whose dimensions were the same, she could be distinguished from them externally by a more built up bridge front.

In 1931 she was converted to burn oil fuel and her funnels were shorn of their traditional cowls and were repainted with black tops.

On 9 August 1937 she had to be beached in Dunkirk outer harbour after being rammed in fog by the cargo steamer *Clan MacNeil* and holed on the port side just abaft the bridge.

She survived World War 2 and afterwards was used as an accommodation ship for Belgian marines at Ostend until broken up in 1947.

Below: *Princesse Marie-Jose* **was the first geared turbine driven Belgian steamer. She could be distinguished from the other ships by her towering bridge front.** *Author's Collection*

Left: *Princesse Marie-Jose* **pictured at Ostend in July 1946 whilst in use as a floating barracks.** *A. M. S. Russell*

Prinses Astrid, Prince Leopold, Prince Charles, Prinses Josephine Charlotte

With an eye to the 1930 Antwerp and Liege Exhibitions the first pair of four new twin-screw steamers was ordered by the Belgium Government in 1928. *Prinses Astrid* was launched by her namesake at Hoboken on 20 July 1929 and *Prince Leopold* on 19 November. A repeat order led to *Prince Charles* and *Princess Josephine Charlotte* following in 1930. These four ships were identical and as can be seen from the following particulars were considerably larger than their forbears:

Length: 347ft 0in
Breadth: 46ft 2in
Depth: 22ft 9in
Gross tonnage: 3,088
Machinery: Two sets single reduction geared turbines

Boilers: Six Babcock & Wilcox w/t 355lb/sq in
Power: 15,400shp
Speed: 23.5kts (contract)

As well as a new more beamy hull design these ships had much more superstructure than earlier ships, the front of which rose in steps to a bridge placed one deck higher than before and which almost dwarfed the two black topped rimless funnels which were made to look even shorter by the raising of the boats on gravity davits.

Below: Prinses Astrid backing alongside the Admiralty Pier at Dover. Her funnels are dwarfed by the massive terraced bridge front. IA Library

Economy of operation was helped by higher boiler pressure and superheating whilst in the accommodation more accent was put on comfort for the 1,425 passengers.

Prince Charles paid a visit to the pool of London in 1931 with members of the Ligue Maritime Belge and she and her sisters performed successfully throughout the 1930s.

Following the outbreak of war, Dover was taken over by the Navy and a single daily service from Folkestone was maintained for a while before all four ships were sent to Southampton for conversion to hospital ships. However the Admiralty changed their minds and they became infantry landing ships instead, being fitted with eight landing craft carried in large gravity davits. *Prince Charles* and *Prince Leopold* were altered at the Royal Dockyard, Devonport whilst the other two sisters were dealt with by Messrs, Silley Cox at Falmouth in January 1941.

In their new guise they put ashore troops at the North African and Salerno landings and later played a not inconsiderable part in the invasion of Normandy. During the latter campaign *Prince Leopold* was torpedoed and sunk south-east of the Nab Tower on 29 July 1944.

In 1945 *Princess Josephine Charlotte* was one of the ships assigned to the relief of Jersey and a year later returned to her peacetime service with the two other surviving ships.

On 22 June 1949 *Prinses Astrid* had the misfortune to strike an old wartime mine about four miles off Dunkirk with the loss of five lives. She sank in Dunkirk roads with just her masts and funnels above water and salvage attempts were abandoned on 20 July after her keel had broken in two.

Princess Josephine Charlotte was sold for scrap to L. Engelen in November 1950 and was towed to their yard at Boom the following month. The sole surviving sister *Prince Charles* remained as the last turbine steamer in the Belgian fleet for a further 10 years before going for scrap to O. Butens who commenced demolition at Hoboken on 21 December 1960.

Prince Baudouin, Prins Albert, Prince Philippe (1940)

Requiring further modern tonnage early in the 1930s the Belgian Marine Administration invited offers from several European shipyards. However the faithful Cockerill concern won the contract for a new ship in the face of competitive tenders from British, French, Dutch and German yards. She was originally to be basically a faster version of the earlier steamers but M. Grimard, the technical adviser to the Administration, had other ideas and backed by the Director-General, M. de Vos, managed to change the contract to a motor ship of his own design.

The *Prince Baudouin* underwent a 17hr trial on 2 August 1934 and on her speed trial on an 11.6-mile deepwater course between the Outer Ruytingen and West Hinder buoys she reached an average of 25.5kts which was a world record for motor driven ships. Some 10ft longer than her predecessors and finer in hull form she had the following main particulars:

Length (oa): 370ft 9in
Breadth: 45ft 11in
Depth/Draught: 16ft 7in/11ft 2in
Gross tonnage: 3,300
Machinery: Two 12-cylinder single acting
Cockerill-Sulzer diesels
Power: 15,000bhp (service)
17,000bhp (maximum continuous)
Speed: 23.5kts (contract)

She introduced an entirely new profile to the Dover Strait with her squat, elliptical funnel and short upright masts, rake being thought unnecessary by her designer. Her large superstructure was more enclosed than hitherto with many large windows, some of which were of toughened glass and which faced forward for the first time. Her accommodation and open deck space catered for a maximum of about 1,700 passengers carried in two classes.

Although not the first motor driven cross-Channel ship to be built, this title having gone to the 1929 built trio for Belfast Steamship Co's 17kt Irish Sea service, *Prince Baudouin* was the first on the English Channel and demonstrated that this method of propulsion was a practical proposition for fast ships whose hulls were by tradition lightly constructed due to draught limitations.

The high power installed was deemed necessary because the Ostend route was longer than the competing Calais and Boulogne ones and much of it lay over shallow sandbanks which had to be circumnavigated at low water.

Although initially more expensive than the turbine the diesel machinery fully justified itself in service by its economical operation and unlike the turbine could be completely shut down when the ship was in port.

A near sister ship *Prins Albert* was launched by the King of the Belgians at Hoboken on 23 April 1937 in a joint ceremony with the cargo liner *Moanda*. On trials in

September she proved to be fractionally the faster of the two by reaching 25.5kts and thereby claimed the world record. A 30% saving in engine room space due to the adoption of main engine driven scavenge pumps in place of the earlier ship's independent electrically driven ones allowed the carriage of an extra hundred or so passengers in more extensive second class accommodation.

A third ship *Prince Philippe* was under construction when war was declared in 1939 and when the Germans invaded in May 1940 only one engine had been completely installed, however she managed to escape to England. She differed from the earlier ships in having a longer bridge and more windows in her first class verandah.

With Dover in Admiralty hands *Prince Baudouin* and *Prins Albert* ran intermittently to Folkestone until 7 May 1940 when the service was suspended. They left Ostend ᶠor the last time on the 18th of the same month bound for

Le Havre with refugees and later joined the rest of the fleet at Southampton. Plans for their conversion to hospital ships were shelved by the Admiralty and they were requisitioned for air target use in July. In 1941 *Prins Albert* and *Prince Philippe* were converted to infantry landing ships at Penarth and the latter was sunk on 15 July 1941 following a collision with the cargo ship *Empire Wave* off the west coast of Scotland.

Prins Albert's war career was long and successful earning her the nickname 'Lucky Albert'. She was present at the Lofoten, Bruneval and Dieppe raids and the North African and Italian landings, later taking part in the Normandy invasion. She then returned to the Mediterranean for the landings in the South of France and at the end of the war was in Singapore. Her sister *Prince Baudouin* was also being prepared for service against the Japanese having been converted to a landing ship by R. & H. Green & Silley Weir at Tilbury in October 1943.

Following their release in 1946 both ships were refitted by Cockerills and returned to normal service though initially they ran to Folkestone until Dover was released by the Admiralty. Their successful service throughout the 1950s and early 1960s provided further proof of the soundness of the original design.

Prince Baudouin was the first to be disposed of in 1964, becoming a floating office and accommodation ship for construction workers at the Zelzate steel works on the Ghent-Terneuzen canal. *Prins Albert* was successively downgraded as new tonnage entered the fleet and was eventually laid up at Ostend as a dead ship in 1969. She was sold for scrap in April the following year to Van Heyghen Freres S.A. who started work on 21 June.

Koning Albert, Prince Philippe (1949)

To replace the two ships lost during the war two further motor ships were put in hand at Hoboken, work on the first having started in great secrecy towards the end of the German occupation. Named *Koning Albert* she was launched on 11 June 1946 in the centenary year of the Ostend service and entered service in January 1948. Her sister *Prince Philippe* followed some six months later, her name perpetuating the 1941 war loss.

Although broadly following the same lines as the prewar motor ships they were slightly larger in dimension and extensive use was made of welding in the construction of their hulls. Their main particulars were as follows:

Length (oa): 372ft 6in
Breadth: 49ft 1in
Depth/Draught: 24ft 5in/12ft 5.25in
Gross tonnage: 3,774
Machinery: Two 12-cylinder single acting Cockerill-Sulzer diesels
Power: 17,000bhp (maximum continuous)
Speed: 25.5kts (trials)

They had two continuous decks, a raked stem and cruiser stern, and were fitted with the obligatory bow rudder to facilitate stern first entry to both terminal ports. Accommodation included two de-luxe two-berth suites, 21 double cabins and 212 sofa-beds in four saloons, whilst public rooms included a totally enclosed first class verandah up forward and restaurants and lounges in both classes. Total daytime passenger complement was about 1,700.

Their machinery arrangement was the same as that installed in *Prins Albert* and their long, lean profiles were to become a familiar sight in the Dover Strait over the next quarter century.

On 16 June 1964 *Koning Albert* collided with the Norwegian tanker *Prometheus* about half way to Ostend and was escorted back to Dover by her sister with extensively damaged bows. On the evening of 30 May 1966 fire broke out in the seamen's quarters of *Prince Philippe* whilst berthed at Ostend, causing considerable damage before being extinguished some three hours later. No passengers were aboard at the time.

Prince Philippe became surplus to requirements in

1973 and was transferred to the Baltic under the management of Stromma, Belgium NV. Renamed *Stromma Rex* she ran between Norrkoping and Mariehamn until 2 September when she caught fire following an engine room explosion. Considered not worth repairing she was sold for scrap and was towed to the Ystad yard of Carl Person where work commenced on 15 November.

Koning Albert meanwhile had lain in Ostend as a reserve ship since 1973 and when her survey became overdue in December 1976 she was put up for sale. She was bought by Van Heyghen Freres and arrived at their Ghent yard for scrapping on 23 May 1978. She had been the thirtieth ship built for the service by Cockerills and fittingly her career had lasted for the same number of years.

Top: The centenary ship *Koning Albert* was much more substantial looking than the prewar motorships through having more of her superstructure enclosed and a wider funnel. Her mainmast was placed unusually far aft. *John G. Callis*

Above: An aerial view of *Koning Albert*. *Skyfotos*

Right: *Prince Philippe* makes a fine sight as she backs towards Dover's western entrance. The slightly projecting bridge cabs gave an unrestricted view when docking stern first. *Author*

Roi Leopold III, Koningin Elisabeth, Reine Astrid

In 1954 the Belgian Marine Administration ordered three new passenger motor ships from Cockerill-Ougree in anticipation of an increase in traffic in connection with the World Exhibition to be held in Brussels in 1958. Although basically similar to the previous ships they nevertheless incorporated several advances in styling, notably tripod masts and a new Lascroux type funnel with sloping top and large vents at either end to promote the dispersal of exhaust fumes. To reduce top weight, aluminium was used in the construction of the funnel, bridge and A deck superstructure.

The new ships were delivered in July 1956, autumn 1957 and May 1958 and their respective 'royal' names were *Roi Leopold III*, *Koningin Elisabeth* and *Reine Astrid*. They shared the following main dimensions:

Length (oa): 373ft 8in
Breadth: 46ft 7in
Depth/Draught: 24ft 9in/12ft 5in
Gross tonnage: 3,795
Machinery: Two 12-cylinder single acting
Cockerill-Sulzer diesels
Power: 15,000bhp (service)
Speed: 23.5kts (designed)

Although almost identical in appearance and dimension the third ship differed from her sisters in being the first Belgian Channel ship to be fitted with stabilisers. Also her accommodation varied slightly in layout from that of the other ships which occupied five decks and included a

Below: Comparison between this profile view of Roi Leopold III and that of Koning Albert reveals the similarity in overall design. Author

verandah bar, two restaurants, smoking room, lounge and four saloons as well as extensive deck space; 18 cabins and 104 saloon berths were fitted and their total passenger complement was around 1,700 carried in two classes. Additionally about 30 cars could be carried in their two holds and two single deck motor coaches on their after deck.

Their main engines were the same 12-cylinder units as those used previously and provided further proof of the success of the original layout. This also meant that maximum use could be made of the interchangeability of spare parts.

The three sister ships together formed the mainstay of the Ostend-Dover passenger service for about 20 years, but after 1968 they altered their English terminal to Folkestone for a while and latterly could occasionally be seen at the end of Southend pier on day shopping excursions from Ostend. In 1973 they reappeared from their winter refits in the new Belgian Sealink livery.

As the emphasis on vehicular traffic increased the two unstabilised ships, which had proved somewhat lively in winter service, were downgraded and by 1975 were only operating on summer weekends and special sailings. Both were disposed of in 1978, *Roi Leopold III* to the Jeddah based Najd Shipping Co who renamed her *Najd* whilst *Koningin Elisabeth* became the *Abha* of Abha Marine Co Ltd, Limassol. *Najd* was converted to roll-on, roll-off operation and between them they operate a Red Sea service between Jeddah, Aquaba and Port Suez. Suggestions that the two companies are jointly-owned, possibly by Greek principals, have been recently confirmed by the reported renaming of *Abha* to *Najd II* in 1979.

At present *Reine Astrid* continues on her original service but is mainly confined to summer relief work and 1980 could well prove to be her last season.

Right: A fine aerial photograph of *Roi Leopold III* on trials showing her deck space and trunked after hatch. *Skyfotos*

Below: *Koningin Elisabeth* picks up speed as she leaves the white cliffs of Dover behind. *Skyfotos*

Bottom: *Reine Astrid* in May 1974 showing the adverse effect in her appearance following the changeover to the Belgian administration's new colour scheme of pale yellow funnel with blue RTM monogram outlined in black. Note the slightly different arrangement of stanchions under the boat deck which distinguished her from her sisters. *Author*

Prinses Paola

The ninth passenger and mail carrying motor ship to be built by Cockerills for the Belgian Marine Administration entered service in 1966. Named *Prinses Paola* she represents the peak of achievement in cross-Channel passenger ferry design and is probably the last of her type to be built anywhere in the world.

From her dimensions tabled beneath it can be seen that she was some 550ton larger than her predecessors and just eclipsed *Invicta* to become the largest ever pure passenger ship on the Channel:

Length (oa): 394ft 3in
Breadth: 52ft 1in
Depth/Draught: 25ft 6in/12ft 6in
Gross tonnage: 4,356
Machinery: Two 12-cylinder turbo-charged Cockerill Sulzer diesels
Power: 15,000bhp (service)
Speed: 22kts (service)

Arguably the best looking of all cross-Channel passenger ships her styling differed from the earlier Belgian trio by reason of a more heavily raked stem, an almost totally enclosed superstructure with different window arrangement and a more streamlined funnel, whilst her tripod masts were raked in sympathy with the leading edge of her funnel. Other differences included fewer lifeboats, much use being made of inflatable liferafts for the first time.

Her propelling machinery broke from the pattern that had been maintained since 1934 and she was the first vessel in the fleet to be fitted with turbocharged units and the first passenger ship in the world to employ the then new Sulzer RD44 engines.

Great attention was paid to passenger comfort with the provision of stabilisers and air-conditioning in all public rooms. Her accommodation ranged over six decks, including an upper sun deck, and out of a total of 1,700 passengers, 600 could enjoy first class facilities which included two de luxe and six special cabins and a verandah bar with large windows facing forward.

She made her first crossing in 1966 and has served the Ostend-Dover route ever since. She was repainted in the new RTM Sealink colours in the winter of 1974 and at the time of writing is maintaining a summer service only, her winter operation being confined to bank holiday and special sailings.

Discussions concerning the replacement of their passenger ships with hovercraft or Boeing jetfoils have been occupying the Belgian Authorities for a while now and news is just to hand that they have opted for a pair of the latter. As a result of this decision there seems little doubt that the Channel days of this fine ship are numbered. She will almost certainly be the last traditional mail steamer to serve on this old established and well worn route and it is to be hoped that when she finally leaves it she will be sold for further trading so that her splendid profile may be seen on the waters of the world for many years to come.

Below: **Leaving Dover in March 1978 in Sealink colours. Her long upper sun deck provides passengers with a good all round view of the Channel.** *Author*

1853–1898 SER
1864–1898 LCDR
1899–1922 SECR
1923–1947 SR
1948–1962 British Transport Commission (Southern Region)
1963–1978 British Rail Board
1979–to date Sealink UK

Calais-Douvres (1877)

The Victorian era was one of experiment and inception and naturally this applied to the sea and ships as well. A new company calling itself the English Channel Steamship Co had built an experimental twin hulled ship, *Castalia*, in 1874 and in the year following another strange ship named *Bessemer*, which was fitted with a 'swinging saloon' designed to minimise the effect of rolling. Neither ship came up to expectations and by the time a third steamer, another catamaran named *Express*, was completed by A. Leslie & Co of Newcastle in 1877 the company was virtually bankrupt.

Express was bought at a bargain price by the LCDR who had been operating their own ships since 1864 and following trials was renamed *Calais-Douvres*. She was less revolutionary than her two predecessors being basically two conventional hulls joined together by wrought iron girders and therefore justifies her inclusion in this book.

She was the largest Channel steamer in existence at the time and her main particulars were as follows:

Length: 302ft 0in
Breadth: 60ft 0in
Depth: 13ft 9in
Gross tonnage: 1,924
Machinery: Four cylinders direct acting diagonal
Boilers: Circular 28lb/sq in
Power: 600nhp
Speed: 13kts

Her two iron hulls were double ended for ease of entry and exit at Calais where the harbour was too narrow for her to turn, and she was driven by a single large paddle wheel mounted between them. Four funnels were provided, two on each hull.

Her entry into service in May 1878 was greeted with much enthusiasm and initially she was very popular with the travelling public. However she soon proved to be difficult to manoeuvre and her speed of 13kts was not considered fast enough for the day service. Her size precluded her from operating the less patronised night service and she was withdrawn in 1887.

She lay at Tilbury for several years, eventually becoming a coal hulk in the Thames.

Below: A rare photograph of the bizarre-looking twin-hulled *Calais Douvres* under way. *Popperfoto*

Invicta (1882)

This steamer, the first of three to be named after the motto of Kent and also the London, Chatham & Dover Railway Company, marked a return to orthodoxy following the experimental *Calais Douvres*. She was the last Channel steamer to come from the Blackwall Yard of the Thames Iron Works, her engines being built by Maudslay, Son & Field, and she was delivered in 1882.

The largest conventional paddle steamer of her day on the Channel she had two funnels and masts and a double ended hull for ease of manoeuvring in and out of Calais. Her main particulars were as follows:

Length: 312ft 4in
Breadth: 33ft 6in
Depth/Draught: 16ft 0in/8ft 6in
Gross tonnage: 1,197
Machinery: One cylinder direct oscillating
Boilers: Box type return tube 30lb/sq in
Power: 4,000ihp
Speed: 18.5kts (trial)

In April 1888 she stranded near Calais due to heavy weather having shifted the sandbanks. Swept by seas for several days she was eventually pulled clear by five tugs, surprisingly without much damage. She stranded again in the same place in 1894.

In 1896 following an Anglo-French mail sharing agreement she was chartered to the Compagnie du Chemin de Fer du Nord who placed her under the French flag (and ran her with a French crew) for two years until they could build their own ships.

Withdrawn following her return to the Chatham Company she was scrapped in 1899.

Below: The double ended Invicta, *seen in Wellington Dock, Dover, was the largest paddle steamer on the Channel when built.* Author's Collection

Victoria (1886), *Empress* (1887)

As a follow up to *Invicta* and to counter increased competition from the SER's ships the Chatham Company ordered two new steamers though this time they chose to build with the Fairfield Shipbuilding & Engineering Company of Govan, near Glasgow. Though not strictly sisters the new ships were very similar in looks and can be taken together. *Victoria* was delivered in 1886 and the larger and faster *Empress* a year later, their names being typical of that era. They had the following main particulars, *Empress* in brackets:

Length: 309ft 4in (324ft 6in)
Breadth: 34ft 1in (34ft 9in)
Depth: 12ft 8in (13ft 5in)
Gross tonnage: 1,030 (1,213)
Machinery: Two cylinder compound diagonal
Boilers: Two double and two single ended 110lb/sq in
Power: 4,720 (6,000ihp)
Speed: 18kts (19.5kts, 20.4kts trials)

Operating on their owners' Calais-Dover service both

ships continued the design pattern introduced by *Invicta*, namely deep double-ended hulls, two masts and twin funnels though they were the first to adopt the narrow black tops which were later to become synonomous with the Company's ships.

In January 1895 whilst entering Calais in a strong north-easterly gale *Empress* was swept onto the west pier damaging her starboard paddle box and losing part of her bridge. She was swept on to the beach about 300yd west of Calais but due to her flat bottom grounded easily and was later towed off. Whilst being repaired the opportunity was taken to reboiler her. Her best crossing was believed to be a fraction of a minute under the hour.

In 1896 *Victoria* was chartered along with *Invicta* to the Chemin de Fer du Nord of France for a period of two years. Made redundant by the new turbine ships she was withdrawn and scrapped by the Shipbreaking Co Ltd in 1904.

In the summer of 1905 *Empress* inaugurated SECR day excursions from Margate to Boulogne three times a week but was sold to breakers the following April. She was replaced for the 1906 season by the more modern paddler *Calais* or the new turbine steamer *Invicta* with additional calls at Dunkirk and Calais but the excursion service was discontinued after 1907.

Below: Victoria **leaving Boulogne showing clearly her canoe-type stern and thin black funnel tops peculiar to the London, Chatham & Dover Railway.** *Author's Collection*

Bottom: Empress **pictured backing out of Calais was very similar to** *Victoria* **but her funnels were of slightly larger diameter. Notice the courtesy tricolour between her funnels.** *Author's Collection*

Calais-Douvres (1889)

Ordered with an eye to the anticipated extra traffic in connection with the 1889 Paris Exhibition this fine paddle steamer resurrected the name of the LCDR's unsuccessful catamaran. She was launched at Fairfield's Govan shipyard on the Clyde in April of that year and later recorded a speed of 21.75kts on the Skelmorlie measured mile. Her main dimensions were as follows:

Length: 324ft 5in
Breadth: 35ft 9in
Depth/Draught: 13ft 5in/8ft 6in
Gross tonnage: 1,212
Machinery: Two sets diagonal direct acting compound
Boilers: Four double ended 110lb/sq in
Power: 6,450ihp
Speed: 20kts (service)

A handsome ship with two raking horizontal-topped funnels she retained the double ended hull which by now was one of the recognisable hallmarks of the Chatham Co's ships along with their distinctive narrow black funnel tops. Her fastest crossing between the ports whose name she bore was recorded as 57min which is equal to a speed of about 22.5kts, and she was the first of the Company's ships to be electrically lit throughout.

Shortly after the rationalisation of the two rival railway companies' services in 1899 she became surplus to requirements and in 1900 was sold to Liverpool & Douglas Steamers which had been set up by a Mr Higginbottom in opposition to the established Packet Company. The service was shortlived being wound up after the death of its owner and *Calais-Douvres* passed in 1903 to the Isle of Man Company who gave her the more appropriate name of *Mona*. She served these owners for a further six years before being broken up at Briton Ferry in 1909.

Above: A powerful study of *Calais Douvres* still steaming hard as she enters the breakwaters at Calais. She differed from the previous Fairfield-built ships in having two prominent ventilators in front of her forward funnel.
Col R. C. Gabriel Collection

Left: *Calais Douvres* in later life as the Isle of Man steamer *Mona* with the addition of a rudimentary bridge.
Author's Collection

Dover, Calais, Lord Warden

In May 1895 the LCDR placed an order with Denny Bros for two new paddle steamers to replace their small 30-year old ships on the Dover-Calais night service. The contract stipulated a speed of 18kts whilst drawing 8.5ft and employing forced draught during one month's actual operation, with delivery dates being set a month apart on 29 January and February 1896.

The first ship was named *Dover* at her launch on 2 December and on 20 January her sister was christened *Calais*. During trials they reached average speeds of 19.36kts and 19.65kts respectively and their main particulars were as follows:

Length: 280ft 0in
Breadth: 35ft 0in
Depth/Draught: 13ft 4in/9ft 11in
Gross tonnage: 979
Machinery: Three cylinder diagonal 35.5in, 52.5in, 76in x 72in stroke
Boilers: Four single ended return tube 150lb/sq in
Power: 4,084ihp
Speed: 18.5kts

The skill of the shipbuilder was vindicated when *Dover* maintained an average speed of 18.6kts during her first month on the Dover-Calais run and both ships used only 13ton of coal per round trip which was less than half the amount used by their predecessors. Delighted with their performance the railway company quickly ordered a third ship and *Lord Warden* was duly delivered on 1 December 1896.

The new ships followed the LCDR style in having 'double-ended' hulls and their single funnels were given naval-type cowls, however a general lack of sheer gave them a somewhat stiff appearance. What they lacked in looks however they certainly made up for in efficiency and were soon making occasional day crossings in addition to their regular night service.

The introduction of new turbine steamers in the early years of the 20th century rendered them obsolete before their time and they were relegated to lesser duties and excursion sailings. On 12 July 1904 *Lord Warden* was chartered by the French to bring a party of guests to Folkestone for the opening of the new pier extension by the French ambassador.

All three sisters were disposed of in 1911 after only 15 years service, *Dover* and *Lord Warden* going for scrap to Stavanger, Norway and Holland respectively. *Calais* was sold to P. Hattemer for further use as an ocean liner tender at Boulogne and whilst acting in this capacity she was torpedoed and sunk by *U-18* on 26 February 1916.

Overtaken by revolutionary events in the world of marine propulsion whilst still in their prime these ships were nonetheless fine examples of their type and were the last to be built for the LCDR.

Below: A fine close up of *Calais* getting under way.
Author's Collection

Above: *Dover* leaving the port from which she took her name. She and her sisters were the last British paddle-steamers to operate the service to Calais. *Author's Collection*

Left: *Au Revoir,* the former *Calais,* backing into Boulogne during her second career as a tender. This view shows up well her unusual stern arrangement. *Author's Collection*

Albert Victor, Louise Dagmar

At the beginning of the 1880s the SER had been in the shipowning business for nearly 30 years after absorbing the fleets of two smaller companies. During this period their ships had evolved from what amounted to no more than steam-propelled sailing ships through a class of eight more substantial single funnelled steamers to the handsome twin stacked clipper bowed *Victoria* of 1861, the latter being the first built to their order. Four more similar ships followed in quick succession.

By the end of 1879 the youngest of these ships was getting on for 15 years old and increasing competition from the rival LCDR led the South Eastern to order two new superior sister ships from the Thames yard of Samuda Bros for their Folkestone-Boulogne service. The first ship, *Albert Victor*, was launched at Poplar on 10 May 1880 by Princess Mary of Teck being tried on 29 June off Maplin where she recorded a mean speed of 18.58kts over six runs. Proceeding to Folkestone she made a special trial crossing on 7 August recording times of 1hr 29.5min outward and 1hr 25min on the return, it being hoped to reduce these by a further 10min or so in service.

The second vessel *Louise Dagmar* was launched on 24 July by Lady Watkin, the wife of the Railway Company's chairman and the main particulars of both ships were as follows:

Length: 250ft 0in
Breadth: 29ft 2in
Depth of hold: 15ft 6in
Gross tonnage: 782
Machinery: One cylinder simple oscillating
Power: 2,800ihp
Speed: 16kts (service)

They were the first steel ships built for the company and the first to have bow rudders. Their foredeck was covered by a light turtle back foc'sle and their funnels had bell mouth tops. Their total passenger capacity was about 600.

From 1 April 1885 fixed schedule running became possible for the first time following the deepening of Boulogne harbour, sailings having previously been dependent on tides. On 7 April 1893 *Louise Dagmar*

Above: No doubt the stokers were shovelling furiously when this photograph of *Louise Dagmar* was taken as she left Boulogne towards the end of the last century. *Col R. C. Gabriel Collection*

Right: Watched by a crowd of interested Victorian spectators *Albert Victor* starts a Channel crossing from Folkestone. This view shows up well the bell-topped funnels favoured by the SER. *Newhaven and Seaford Historical Society*

outward bound from Boulogne collided with the French ship *Alberte* and damaged her bows necessitating 10 days' repairs at the Thames shipyard of R. & H. Green.

Becoming surplus to requirements upon the amalgamation of the two rival companies on 1 January 1899 both ships were sold for scrap the following March.

Duchess of Edinburgh

A further passenger steamer, *Duchess of Edinburgh*, was ordered by the SER in 1880 but this time they turned to the well known Clydebank firm of Messrs J. & G. Thomson (later to become even better known as John Brown & Co). A steel paddler of similar dimensions to the Samuda built pair but with compound engines for higher speed she was launched on 21 July.

Her trials on the Clyde on 12 October produced a rather disappointing average speed of 17.68kts over six runs. Indeed she was never a success and made only a few trips from Folkestone following her arrival there on 14 May 1881. In August 1882 her lay up berth was changed from Folkestone to Sheerness and shortly afterwards she was sold to J. Little & Co of Barrow who ran her (from

there) to the Isle of Man, renaming her *Manx Queen* the following year. She was chartered to the Belgian government for a while sometime in 1888/9 as a stand-in on the Ostend-Dover service for their unsatisfactory new *Prince Albert* which had had to return to her builders for extensive alteration.

Passing to the Midland Railway in 1905 she was reboilered and after another two years' service was eventually sold to Messrs J. J. King of Garston for scrap.

Above: The unsatisfactory *Duchess of Edinburgh* was sold after only a short career on the English Channel to become the Barrow SN CO's *Manx Queen*. This view shows her leaving Douglas, Isle of Man after lengthening and with bell funnel tops removed. *Author's Collection*

Mary Beatrice

A new ship was needed to replace the unsuccessful *Duchess of Edinburgh* and it was hardly surprising that the South Eastern Railway returned to Samuda Bros who had been responsible for the satisfactory 1880-built pair of ships.

Mary Beatrice as she became known was completed in 1882 and was basically a repeat of the *Albert Victor*

Below: *Mary Beatrice* lying in Folkestone Harbour. *Folkestone Central Library.*

design but with an extra five feet in length which raised her gross tonnage to 803. In all other respects she was identical to the earlier pair and she made her first crossing from Folkestone on 19 August.

Her performance in service carrying up to 625 passengers must have been entirely satisfactory as little is written about her and her career seems to have been singularly without incident.

Following a major refit in 1898 she emerged without the familiar bell tops to her funnels but her new image was shortlived for she became surplus to requirements a year after the merger with the LCDR and after lying alongside the Admiralty Pier at Dover for a while was sold for scrap in January 1900.

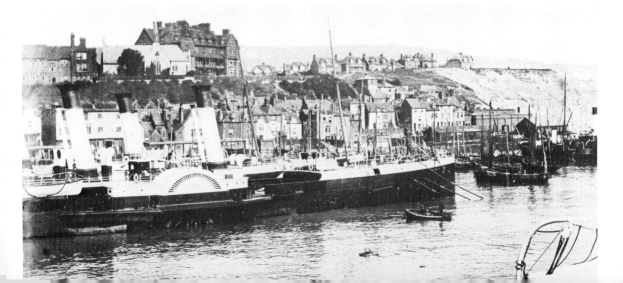

Duchess of York, Princess of Wales

In spite of declining passenger traffic on the Folkestone route, due to intense competition from the newer London, Chatham and Dover ships, the SER ordered a new steamer from R. & H. Green of London. Named *Duchess of York* she was completed in 1895 and was the last Channel steamer to be built on the Thames.

A fine looking ship with two bell-topped funnels, she was more substantial looking than the earlier ships and differed from them in having compound diagonal engines with one high pressure and two low pressure cylinders built by John Penn & Sons.

However looks are not everything and she must have suffered from mechanical problems for as soon as she arrived at Folkestone in August she had to return to her builders. There she remained until 22 May 1897. On 2 June amidst great pomp she made her much delayed maiden voyage, at the same time inaugurating a new afternoon service which connected with a new express train to Paris. Although this was an instant success and passenger figures rose to record heights further doubts remain as to her own satisfaction, reinforced by the fact that a second new ship was ordered almost immediately.

Princess of Wales was launched by Lairds of Birkenhead on 21 May 1898 by Miss Boxer, the daughter of the Railway Company's marine superintendent, and carried out speed trials on 8 October, achieving an average of 19.1kts.

Below: *Duchess of York* **leaving Folkestone. The five portholes and fan-like vents on her paddle box are recognition features** *Folkestone Central Library*

The main particulars of both ships were as follows (*Duchess of York* figures first):

Length: 270ft 0in
Breadth: 30ft 0in/32ft 2in
Depth: 14ft 6in/15ft 5in
Gross tonnage: 996/1,009
Machinery: Three cylinder compound diagonal
Boilers: Four SE
Power: 684nhp/740nhp (4,000ihp)
Speed: 18.5kts/19kts

The new ship entered service in the late autumn of 1898 and settled down on the Boulogne run for the next few years, though she was perhaps a little extravagant on coal, burning 18 tons per trip.

In November 1904 *Duchess of York* was sold to breakers in Holland after only seven years service, though her duties latterly had amounted to nothing more than cheap coastal cruises.

With the coming of the turbine steamers *Princess of Wales* was forced into reserve, on one occasion her saloon bulkhead being broken by a rogue wave whilst standing in for the damaged *Empress* during a strong gale on the last day of August 1908. The following year saw her making cheap day excursions to Boulogne on summer Mondays.

Finally eclipsed by the turbines she was sold in 1910 to S. Lambrus-chini Ltd of Buenos Aires who renamed her *Rio Uruguay*, fitted her with radio, and placed her on the Plate estuary service to Montevideo. In 1921 she was bought by C. Pujol and she was eventually broken up in 1930 after a career of 32 years during which she had served for almost equal periods in separate hemispheres.

Mabel Grace

Just before the merging of the services of the two railway companies on 1 January 1899 the South Eastern had ordered yet another new steamer from Laird Bros. She was built to the maximum dimensions then permitted to enter Boulogne and ran trials in Wemyss Bay on 2 September 1899, achieving a mean rate of 20.23kts during the course of six runs.

Her main particulars were:

Length: 300ft 0in
Breadth: 36ft 1in
Depth: 15ft 4in
Gross tonnage: 1,315
Machinery: Three cylinder compound diagonal
Boilers: Six return tube 120lb/sq in
Power: 5,500ihp
Speed: 20kts

An extremely handsome ship *Mabel Grace* broke completely with company tradition in having two rather short, widely spaced funnels with deep black tops and no bell mouths, however she did retain the turtle back foc'sle. When delivered her bridge was placed between the funnels but a wheelhouse was later added in front of the forward stack. She could accommodate 230 passengers on her comfortable promenade deck and a further 500 in saloons and private cabins.

Mabel Grace arrived at Folkestone for the first time on 19 September and after making a trial crossing on 21st entered service the following day.

Sadly her career, so full of promise, was cut short by the rapid switch to turbine propulsion, this being achieved on the Dover Strait without the interim recourse to reciprocating engines found necessary on other routes. With an unblemished record she was sold for scrapping in 1909, passing into the history books as the last proponent of the paddle wheel to be built for regular cross-Channel service.

The Queen, Onward, Invicta (1905), Victoria (1907), Empress (1907)

Following upon the success of the world's first turbine driven passenger steamers William Denny & Son, their builder, approached the South Eastern and Chatham managing committee with the offer of a similarly propelled channel steamer. the Company agreed and the ship was put in hand at Dumbarton, being launched on 4 April 1903 and named *The Queen*. She underwent extensive trials in May during the course of which she obtained a mean speed of 21.73kts on the Skelmorlie mile. Her astern speed was 13kts and her manoeuvrability was such that she was brought to a dead stop from 19kts in 1min 7sec in less than 2½ times her own length.

A ship of pleasing proportions with two elegantly raking funnels capped with unobtrusive cowls and tall raking steel masts, she had the following main particulars:

Length: 323ft 0in
Breadth: 40ft 0in
Depth/Draught: 16ft 6in/13ft 10in
Gross tonnage: 1,676
Machinery: Three Parsons turbines (One HP and two LP) driving three shafts
Boilers: Two double ended and two single ended 150lb/sq in

Above: *The Queen* was the world's first turbine-driven Channel steamer. *Author's Collection*

Left: *Onward* leaving the port of Folkestone where she was a regular caller. In 1908 she became the first Channel steamer to carry the occasional motor car and one can be seen on her foredeck. *Author's Collection*

Below: The elegance of Denny's design is well portrayed in this trials view of *Invicta*. *Author's Collection*

Right: *Empress* in dazzle paint whilst serving as a seaplane carrier in World War I. *Author's Collection*

Below: The long-lived *Victoria* shown during her second career with the Isle of Man Steam Packet Co. *Author's Collection*

Power: 7,500ihp
Speed: 21kts

Passenger accommodation was arranged on two decks, first class on the awning deck and second class on the main deck abaft the engine room. The latter followed the principle adopted in the pioneer ships of a high pressure centre turbine exhausting into two low pressure wing turbines which were also used for going astern, all three driving individual shafts directly. Her outer shafts were built with two screws apiece but one was later removed.

The Queen entered service on 29 June 1903 and the success of her first year in operation, during which she averaged 21kts, was such that Denny's were given a repeat order for two more ships with only minor improvements. Named *Onward* and *Invicta* they were delivered on 27 April and 3 July, 1905 and were fitted with an automatic device which allowed all watertight

doors to be closed from the bridge in only 14sec. Almost exactly two years later in April and June 1907 a second pair of repeat sister ships were handed over, being named *Victoria* and *Empress*.

The SECR had thus received in only four years five new ships that were amongst the finest of their type in the world. As far as routeing was concerned the five were virtually interchangeable though *The Queen* and *Onward* became particularly associated with the Folkestone-Boulogne service from 1907 until World War 1 and on 30 May 1908 they collided head-on with each other in patchy fog in mid-Channel, one lookout on *Onward* being killed. Both sustained bow damage.

Upon the outbreak of war the first four ships were pressed into service as transports between South Coast ports and France and on 26 October 1914 *The Queen* rescued 2,200 refugees from the torpedoed French steamer *Amiral Ganteaume*. Some two years later on 26

August 1916 she was surprised by a raiding flotilla of German destroyers near the Varne bank and was scuttled by a boarding party after the crew had been allowed to leave in the boats. The fifth and newest sister *Empress* had meanwhile been converted to a seaplane carrier, with armoured belting and a large hangar aft, and as such spent almost three years abroad in West African, Mediterranean and Red Sea waters.

Soon after resuming normal service *Invicta* and *Empress* were sold in June 1923 to the French SAGA group as replacements for their paddlers *Le Nord* and *Pas de Calais*. Refitted at Calais and Dover respectively and with white funnels once more they served their new owners for a further ten years before being sold for scrap in April 1933.

The two remaining ships both went to the Isle of Man Steam Packet Co but with an eight-year interval between their sales. *Onward* had caught fire at Folkestone on 24 September 1918 and was scuttled clear of the quay to extinguish the flames. Raised within a month by means of an array of winches and five railway engines she was towed to London for repair. She was bought by the Isle

of Man Company following reconditioning by Fletcher, Son & Fearnall in Union Dock, Limehouse and made her first trip from Liverpool to Douglas on 22 May 1920, being renamed *Monas Isle* that August. In March 1928 the same company took *Victoria* for their Heysham service subsequently converting her to oil-firing in 1932.

When war came again in 1939 *Monas Isle* was used as an armed boarding vessel in the North Sea, later being severely damaged at Dunkirk. After repairs she became an AA guard ship off the north-east coast and ended the war as a naval accommodation ship. Released in June 1945 minus her mainmast she completed another three seasons before being sold for scrapping at Milford Haven by T. W. Ward in 1948.

Victoria meanwhile had continued in service until she hit a mine off the Mersey Bar lightvessel on 21 December 1940. Repaired by Cammell Lairds she was requisitioned for conversion to an infantry landing ship, being released again in 1946. She completed a further 10 years on Isle of Man service before passing into the hands of shipbreakers T. W. Ward at Barrow in January 1957.

Riviera, Engadine

The SECR ordered a further new turbine steamer from Denny Bros on 9 June 1910. She was to be a repeat of the previous pair but with an extra half knot in speed as well as other alterations and with a six-month option on a sister ship, which was taken up after the shipyard had granted an extension. Both ships were named after well known holiday areas and the first, *Riviera*, was launched on 1 April 1911. Having reached 23.03kts on the measured mile she was delivered at Dumbarton on 7 June. Her sister *Engadine* took to the water on 23 September and their main dimensions were as follows:

Length: 316ft 0in
Breadth: 41ft 1in
Depth/Draught: 16ft 5in/14ft 2.25in

Gross tonnage: 1,675
Machinery: Three sets Parsons geared turbines
Boilers: Six Babcock & Wilcox w/t 172lb/sq in
Power: 8,100ihp
Speed: 23kts

Both ships took up station on the Dover-Calais run where they replaced the last surviving London & Chatham paddlers. The main outward difference

Below: Riviera **at speed on trials in the Clyde showing her long, clear afterdeck. She and her South Eastern & Chatham Co sisters had all black funnels from the end of the war until 1923/24 when they adopted the Southern's buff with a black top.** *Author's Collection*

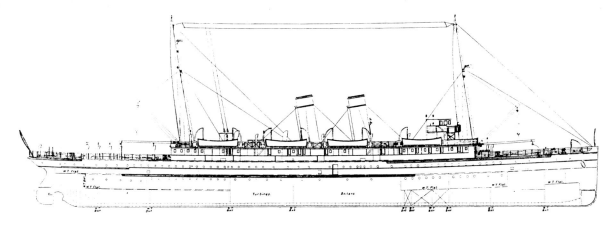

Above left: *Engadine* rebuilt as a seaplane carrier during World War 1. The windage on her large hangar gave rise to steering problems. *IWM*

Centre left: *Engadine* passing Gravesend whilst on charter to Instone Lines in the summer of 1932. Note that her promenade deck has been enclosed.
Laurence Dunn Collection

Bottom left: *Riviera* still retained much of her former elegance as Burns & Lairds Lines' *Lairds Isle* despite postwar alterations to her superstructure. *Author's Collection*

between them and the earlier turbines was a clear after end to both main and awning decks which were strengthened for the carriage of cars, a large hatch being fitted on the latter. Internal innovations included the substitution of water tube boilers for the cylindrical variety. Cabin accommodation was provided for 105 first class and 45 second class passengers.

Taken over by the Admiralty at the beginning of World War 2 they were both temporarily fitted to carry three seaplanes at Chatham. A more substantial conversion to allow the carriage of four aircraft took place a year later, somewhat surprisingly undertaken by Cunard at Liverpool.

Both served subsequently in the North Sea and *Engadine* made history at Jutland when she became the first ship to launch an aircraft during a naval engagement. She later tried to tow the damaged cruiser HMS *Warrior* to port and took off 675 men when the latter sank.

Due to the late release of Dover by the Admiralty and industrial troubles it was 1920 before both ships returned to peacetime service following refits at Chatham. Employed mainly on the Folkestone-Boulogne run they were downgraded in 1925 following the introduction of new ships and spent the next seven years running summer excursions only. In the summer of 1932 with the Depression at its height *Engadine* was chartered to Instone Lines who ran her on a daily return trip from the Pool of London to the Nore lightvessel, her funnels being painted bright yellow during this period. Returning to Dover at the end of September she was laid up and the following year, having been bought by Compania Maritima, made the long voyage out to the Philippines where she was renamed *Corregidor* and placed on a 350-mile inter-island service. Overtaken by war in the Pacific she was mined and sunk in Manila Bay on 17 December 1941, with great loss of life.

Riviera was sold to J. B. Coupar of Glasgow on behalf of HMS *Catherwood* in November 1932 but was resold to Burns Laird Lines Ltd early the following year. Converted to burn oil fuel she was renamed *Laird's Isle* and placed on a summer daytime service between Ardrossan and Belfast. Apart from war service, at first on the Dover Patrol and later as a troop landing ship at D-Day, she remained on this route till 6 August 1957 when she was laid up at Greenock. Two months later she finally went to be broken up at Troon after a long career spanning 46 years of peace and war.

Biarritz, Maid of Orleans (1918)

Embodying all the latest improvements in design this pair of ships represented the final stage of evolution of *The Queen* design. *Biarritz* had been ordered before the outbreak of World War 1 but was not launched until 7 December 1914, running her official trial on 9 March 1915 during which she attained a mean speed of 23.8kts on the Skelmorlie mile.

Her main particulars were:

Length: 341ft 3in
Breadth: 45ft 0in
Depth/Draught: 16ft/12ft 7.5in

Gross tonnage: 2,495 (*M of O* 2,384)
Machinery: Two sets Parsons geared turbines
Boilers: Six Babcock & Wilcox w/t 202lb/sq in
Power: 10,000ihp
Speed: 23kts

Requisitioned by the Admiralty on completion *Biarritz* spent the war years as a minelayer, initially in the North Sea and later in the Mediterranean where her efforts at the entrance to the Dardanelles were instrumental in sinking the German cruiser *Breslau* and damaging the battle cruiser *Goeben*.

Although ordered in August 1914 the construction of the second ship *Maid of Orleans* was delayed and she was taken over by the Admiralty whilst still on the stocks in 1917, being delivered as a transport on 2 August 1918 and making her first voyage between Southampton and Le Havre on the 16th. She was released first and took up her designed Dover-Calais sailings in 1920, being joined by *Biarritz* at the end of 1921 following an extensive refit by Vickers Armstrongs at Barrow. They were the first ships in the Straits to be propelled by geared turbines.

During the winter and spring of 1925/6 both ships underwent three-month refits at Denny's during which they were converted to oil burning, one boiler being removed, and their promenade decks were almost fully enclosed. Following this they commenced running on a year-round service between Folkestone and Boulogne, on which they remained until the outbreak of war in 1939.

Both acted as British Expeditionary Force leave ships between Dover and Boulogne from December until the following May, but with a trip to Rotterdam to pick up Dutch nationals in April. During the Dunkirk evacuation *Biarritz* was badly damaged in her boiler-room by shellfire and had to return to Southampton for repairs, however her sister more than made up for her by lifting over 5,000 men to safety before herself being damaged in collision with a destroyer on 1 June 1940.

Following a spell trooping on the Stranraer-Larne service *Biarritz* was used briefly as a target ship for naval airmen and in 1942 both ships were refitted as landing ships for the Normandy invasion. Whilst returning from the beaches on 28 June *Maid of Orleans* was mined and sank half an hour later with the loss of six crew members.

Biarritz continued trooping in grey livery until overhauled by Denny's at the end of 1947. After that her duties were varied but were mainly confined to troop and displaced person service on the Harwich and Dover routes. With the launch of the new *Maid of Orleans* only a month away she was laid up in Southampton in August 1948 and on 4 November was towed to Dover where she was broken up on the beach by Dover Metal Industries.

In her 34-year career she had served through two world wars and she was the only South Eastern & Chatham Railway ship to become a unit of the British Transport Commission fleet, albeit only briefly.

Isle of Thanet, Maid of Kent

Not long after its formation at the beginning of 1923 the SR turned its attentions to replacing its first line fleet on the short sea routes and during the winter of 1924/5 placed orders with Denny's for two new passenger ships. Launched on 23 April and 5 August 1925 they were named *Isle of Thanet* and *Maid of Kent* respectively and took up their appointed stations in July and November, the former running from Dover to Calais and the latter from Folkestone to Boulogne.

They shared the following main particulars:

Length: 342ft 0in
Breadth: 45ft 0in
Depth/Draught: 17ft 6in/12ft 10in
Gross tonnage: 2,664
Machinery: Two sets single reduction Parsons geared turbines
Boilers: Five Babcock & Wilcox oil-fired w/t 202lb/sq in
Power: 8,500shp
Speed: 22kts (service)

They marked a return to single funnels (the first on the Straits since the three Denny built paddlers of 1896) and also introduced cruiser sterns and enclosed awning decks. Their hulls were subdivided by 13 watertight bulkheads and their accommodation provided for the carriage of 1,000 first class and 400 second class passengers, who benefitted from the extra area of covered deck space.

Both ships were requisitioned at the beginning of the war and after several trooping runs were converted to hospital ships at Southampton. Shortly afterwards on 21 May 1940, whilst assisting in the evacuation of France, *Maid of Kent* was bombed and sunk in Dieppe harbour with the loss of 17 of her crew. Her sister ship survived Dunkirk and later went north to be used as a target ship for the Fleet Air Arm. Early in 1943 she was converted to an infantry landing ship (hand-hoist) and became the headquarters ship for Force J which was made up of similarly converted channel steamers based at Cowes, Isle of Wight, and which took part in the Normandy landings. Towards the end of the war she carried refugees between Southampton and Ostend, and Newhaven and Dieppe.

Refitted on release in 1945 she spent just over a year on the Newhaven run before returning to the Straits in February 1947. Apart from a 10-month spell on the Dover-Boulogne service from 1 July that year she remained on the Folkestone-Calais/Boulogne route until 1963, though latterly on summer day excursions only. She made her final crossing on 15 September and was laid up in Dover. Sold the following year to Hughes

Bolckow & Co Ltd she left in tow for Blyth on 10 June, her 38 years of active service in peace and war having more than made up for the half life of her less fortunate sister.

Canterbury

The advent of a new and prestigious first class train service between London and Paris in May 1927, the famous 'Golden Arrow', called for a suitable steamer to provide the sea link and early in 1928 the *Canterbury* was ordered from Denny Bros by the Southern Railway. Launched at Dumbarton on 13 December 1928 in a high state of completion she left the yard only three months later and was delivered in Southampton on 15 March 1929.

Bearing a strong family resemblance to the two previous ships she had a larger beam as can be seen from her following main measurements:

Length (oa): 341ft 6in
Breadth: 47ft 0in
Depth/Draught: 17ft 9in/12ft 10in
Gross tonnage: 2,912 (3,071 from 1932)
Machinery: Two sets single reduction Parsons geared turbines

Boilers: Four Babcock & Wilcox oil-fired w/t 227lb/sq in
Power: 8,500shp
Speed: 21kts (service)

Her tall funnel and lofty masts of equal rake gave her a well-balanced profile and she created much interest following her introduction on the new service between Dover and Calais on 15 May. Although she was certified to carry up to 1,700 passengers she initially only carried about 300 who enjoyed more luxurious accommodation than anything hitherto which included two suites and 18 private cabins, a restaurant seating about 100 and a 'palm court'.

Bedevilled at first by mechanical problems she underwent an extensive refit during the winter of 1931/32 in the course of which she was given 2nd class accommodation. These were the days of the Depression and the first class only service vanished for ever. In 1935

Above: The graceful *Canterbury* leaving Dover with her Golden Arrow passengers in February 1939: comparatively shallow water accounts for the build up towards her stern. *IA Library*

Left: *Canterbury* exercising in the Channel with Force J prior to the Normandy invasion. Note the lack of mainmast and stowage position of her landing craft. *IWM*

Below: A postwar aerial view of *Canterbury* at speed in the Channel showing the slight alteration to her paint scheme. *Skyfotos*

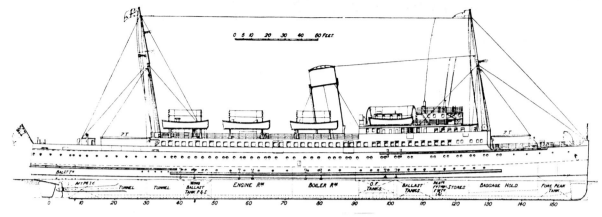

she was present at King George V's Jubilee Naval Review at Spithead.

After the outbreak of war she served as a transport for troops and refugees on a number of routes and later made five trips to Dunkirk between 25 May and 4 June. Following a brief period as a Fleet Air Arm target ship she was transferred to the Larne-Stranraer run on 2 July 1941 and in June the following year was withdrawn for conversion to a troop landing ship at Ardrossan, emerging in February 1943 with six LCAs carried outboard in special hand-hoist davits. She joined Force J made up of similarly converted Channel steamers based at Cowes but whilst returning from a brief visit to Oban she lost two of her starboard landing craft which had filled with water in heavy weather in the Western Channel. After taking part in the Normandy invasion she ran for just over a year as a military leave ship between Calais and Kent ports, after which she was released and refitted by Vickers Armstrong on the Tyne, finally returning to the 'Golden Arrow' run on 15 April 1946.

Replaced by *Invicta* six months later she was switched to the Folkestone-Calais run where she remained, apart from a six-month spell on her old service from January 1947, until moved once again in the summer of 1948 to a seasonal Folkestone-Boulogne service. Here she stayed for the next 16 years, being withdrawn and laid up in Dover after a final crossing on 27 September 1964.

On 30 July 1965 this most popular ship left the port she knew so well for Antwerp in tow of a Belgian tug, there to be stripped of her fittings before being finally demolished by the Brussels Shipbreaking Co at Willebroek.

Invicta (1940)

In February 1939 the SR returned once again to Denny's with an order for a new passenger vessel to take over from the 10-year old *Canterbury* on the 'Golden Arrow' service. War intervened during her construction and she was taken over by the Admiralty, being launched on 14 December. Following her completion on 1 July 1940 she lay at anchor near Clynder on the Clyde for a year until the Admiralty decided to convert her to an assault landing ship, her livery during that period being an overall buff save for a black hull and funnel top.

Fitted with six LCAs held in special davits attached to the side of her superstructure she could accommodate 250 troops and subsequently took part in the Dieppe raid and the Normandy invasion as part of Force J.

Refitted after her release from war service during which she was converted to an oil-burner *Invicta* made her first peacetime crossing from Dover on 15 October 1946. It had originally been intended to fit her with stabilisers but these were omitted due to her rapid construction and were eventually fitted in 1947.

The largest passenger ship on the Channel for many years she had a more built up profile than her predecessors and her main dimensions were as follows:

Length: 348ft 3in
Breadth: 52ft 3in
Depth/Draught: 16ft 5in/12ft 9in
Gross tonnage: 4,178
Machinery: Two sets Parsons single reduction geared turbines
Boilers: Two Yarrow three drum w/t 250lb/sq in
Power: 11,000shp
Speed: 22kts (service)

Top right: The brand new *Invicta* **undergoing conversion to a troop landing ship. Note the gun platforms and special davits fixed to her side for hoisting landing craft.** *IWM*

Centre right: A late 1950s view of *Invicta* **at speed in her peacetime colours.** *Skyfotos*

Right: Leaving Dover in British Rail Sealink colours towards the end of her career. *Author*

She could carry up to 1,400 passengers on four of her five decks, her main and upper decks being continuous and the promenade deck nearly so. In 1962 her accommodation was modernised.

She remained on the Dover-Calais run with the exception of the odd summer extra sailing to Boulogne for nearly 26 years until replaced in the British Rail fleet by the new multi-purpose ferry *Horsa*, and she made her

final sailing on 8 August 1972. Two days later after de-storeing she made her way to Newhaven to be laid up. Some interest was apparently shown in her by a Greek company who were proposing a Brindisi-Patras service but this came to nothing and on 21 September she was towed away by the German tug *Michel Petersen* for demolition at Nieuw Lekkerland by the Dutch shipbreakers 'de Koophandel'.

Maid of Orleans (1949)

Ordered by the SR prior to nationalisation to replace her namesake lost during the war this new steamer became the first to be delivered to the British Transport Commission. Launched on 17 September 1948 by Lady Missenden at Dumbarton she joined *Canterbury* the following year on the Folkestone-Boulogne run, making her first trip on 23 June 1949.

Introducing a pleasing new profile to the Dover Strait the *Maid* had the following main particulars:

Length (oa): 341ft 0in
Breadth: 50ft 0in
Depth/Draught: 18ft/12ft 5.5in
Gross tonnage: 3,776
Machinery: Two sets Parsons single reduction geared
turbines
Boilers: Two Foster Wheeler w/t 280lb/sq in
Power: 11,000shp
Speed: 22kts

Although 20 years younger than *Canterbury* the *Maid*'s outward design, when analysed, was basically the same as the older ship whilst incorporating the advances in ship styling that had evolved in the intervening years

such as a raked stem, wider and shorter funnel, and more built-up superstructure. Stabilisers were fitted for the comfort of her 886 first class and 736 second class passengers and for ease of manoeuvre she had the by now obligatory bow rudder.

She normally ran two day services but these were increased to three in number in 1964, her work load increasing yet further when *Canterbury* was replaced by *St Patrick* the following year. During the winter she usually stood in for *Cote d'Azur* and *Invicta* during their overhauls.

Due to exhaust fume problems her funnel was heightened and fitted with a 'fireman's helmet' type spark arrester during a winter 1958/9 overhaul at Southampton and her second class accommodation was improved during subsequent overhauls in 1962 and 1966.

In the autumn of 1965 plans to convert her to a side loading car ferry for the Fishguard-Rosslare route were discussed and then abandoned.

Below: Maid of Orleans **at full stretch during her trials in the Clyde in the spring of 1949. Designed primarily as a day boat, she had much less superstructure than** *Invicta.*
Laurence Dunn Collection

An unusual sailing from Dover to Boulogne on 8 April 1973 was a foretaste of things to come for on 2 June she was transferred to that port to take up the former 'Golden Arrow' schedule to Calais. This was a summer only service and she operated as a one-class ship.

It was widely expected that the 1974 season would be her last but she reappeared once more in June 1975 before returning to her lay-up berth in Newhaven at the end of September. Sold for scrap she left the Sussex port on 6 November in tow of the Spanish tug *Ibaizabal Tres* and three days later arrived at Santander for the attentions of Steelnorte S. L. San Esteban de Pravia.

Her career of 26 years had been devoid of major incident but she had been a successful ship and was the last of her type built by Denny's to serve the Dover Straits.

Below: A later aerial view showing her heightened funnel with its fireman's helmet top. *Skyfotos*

Bottom: Leaving Dover on 27 July 1974 in full Sealink colours. *Author*

1896–1920 Societe de Chemin de Fer du Nord
1921–1936 Societe Anonyme de Gerance et d'Armament (SAGA)
1936–to date Societe Nationale des Chemins de Fer Francais (SNCF)

Le Nord, Le Pas de Calais

Consequent upon the mail sharing agreement between France and England in 1896, the Chemin de Fer du Nord placed an order for two paddle-driven steamers with the Ateliers et Chantiers de la Loire, St Nazaire, chartering the Chatham Railway paddlers *Invicta* and *Victoria* in the intervening years before their completion. The new ships were far and away the largest paddle steamers built for Channel service and were the only French examples of this type of ship. Both appeared on the Dover-Calais run in 1898 their normal service being the early morning mail run whilst the Chatham Company maintained the midday and night services. Their main dimensions were:

Length: 337ft 8in
Breadth: 35ft 9in
Depth: 14ft 2in
Gross tonnage: 2,004
Machinery: Three-cylinder triple expansion diagonal
Boilers: Lagraffel et d'Allest w/t 186lb/sq in
Power: 8,000shp
Speed: 21.5kts

They were handsome single funnel ships which resembled somewhat the Chatham Company's *Dover* trio, but they were given counter sterns and a wheelhouse placed forward of the funnel. Their original boilers, which were of the water tube type, suffered from constant priming, and in 1911 they were replaced by new lighter ones of the Solignac-Grille type which consumed less coal and gave quicker firing and increased speed.

On 26 May 1910 off Calais *Le Pas de Calais* accidentally rammed and sank the French submarine *Pluviose* which had surfaced suddenly in front of her, all 27 aboard being lost.

Below: *Le Pas de Calais* **backing out of Calais. Note the nice little touch of decoration on her spirket plate.**
Author's Collection

At the start of World War 1 both ships were requisitioned as auxiliary light cruisers in the Second Light Squadron, Channel, but almost immediately, in October, *Le Nord* was lent to the British Red Cross. Between 1916 and 1917 both ships were used as seaplane carriers based at Dunkirk and it was during this period that *Le Nord* rammed and sank a German U-boat.

After the war they were sold in August 1920 to the Societe Anonyme de Gerance et d'Armement, a Rothschild owned company, who continued to run them on the Calais-Dover service. Both met their fate in 1923, *Le Nord* becoming a total loss after stranding near the South Foreland in May, whilst her sister ship went to the breakers the following September.

Empress, Invicta

The Societe de Gérance et d'Armement purchased these two turbine steamers from the South Eastern & Chatham Railways Managing Committee in June 1923 to replace their paddle steamers *Le Nord* and *Le Pas de Calais*. Their histories have already been covered in the British ship section and they were sold for scrap in 1933 after 10 years under the French flag on the Calais-Dover route.

Above: *Empress* arriving at Dover in 1926 whilst under French flag. Note her plated in promenade deck. *Author's Collection*

Left: *Invicta* at Dover whilst on charter to the Chemin de Fer du Nord. *Newhaven and Seaford Historical Society*

Cote d'Azur (1930), *Cote d'Argent*

With *Empress* and *Invicta* nearing the end of their useful life, the Societe Anonyme de Gérance et d'Armement put in hand a replacement programme, ordering two fine new turbine steamers from the F. & C. de la Mediterranee. Named after two well known holiday areas, the first ship, *Cote d'Azur*, was completed in 1930 and her sister, *Cote d'Argent*, some two years later, making her inaugural crossing on 3 April 1932.

The main particulars of both ships were as follows:

Length: 325ft 10in
Breadth: 45ft 0in
Depth: 25ft 0in
Gross tonnage: 3,047/3,049
Machinery: Two sets Parsons single reduction geared turbines
Boilers: Four oil-fired Rauber & Luquet w/t
Power: 14,000shp
Speed: 23kts

Distinctive and near identical ships, they could be distinguished by the differing depths of black paint on their funnel tops. Their accommodation provided for 900 first class passengers with a further 500 second class.

In 1934 SAGA tried to sell them to the Southern Railway but, for reasons of prestige, the sale was vetoed by the French Ministry of Marine. In May 1940, just before Dunkirk, the *Cote d'Azur* was requisitioned to help with the evacuation of troops and refugees from Flushing and Ostend. Whilst similarly engaged at Dunkirk, she was bombed and sunk on the 27 May.

Raised by the Germans in 1941 she was converted into a minelayer and minus her mainmast was deployed in the Baltic under the name of *Ostmark*. On the night of 21 April 1945 she was surprised by RAF Mosquitos just west of Anholt and was sunk.

Her sister meanwhile had been caught by the German advance whilst assisting in the evacuation at La Pallice. Severely damaged she was towed to St Nazaire for repair, at the same time undergoing conversion to a minelayer. Renamed *Elsass* she was eventually mined and sunk off Namsos on 3 June 1944.

Below: These two views of *Cote d'Azur* (below) and *Cote d'Argent* (bottom) show clearly the former's taller funnel with its broader black top. On both ships the funnel top was separated from the white paint by a narrow metal band, that of *Cote d'Azur* being blue, whilst *Cote d'Argent's* was silver in colour. *Author's Collection*

Cote d'Azur (1950)

In 1949 the SNCF ordered a fast new turbine steamer from Le Havre to replace the two SAGA ships which had been lost during World War 2. She was launched at the Graville yard of F. & C. de la Mediteranee on 3 April 1950 and underwent speed trials on the measured mile off Cherbourg on 31 July, attaining more than 25.5kts on two boilers and 20.5kts with only one in operation. She cost around £1,400,000, and her main particulars were as follows:

Length (oa): 364ft 2.5in
Breadth: 48ft 4.5in
Depth: 12ft 3in
Gross tonnage: 3,998
Machinery: Two sets Parsons SR geared turbines
Boilers: Two FCM 47 oil-fired
Power: 22,000shp (max) 16,000shp (normal)
Speed: 24kts (contract) 21.5kts (service)

She was a three-deck ship with considerable sheer, and notable flair forward, and was fitted with a streamlined Strombos type funnel by Valensi, which ensured the efficient dispersal of exhaust gases. Aluminium was used for the first time in the construction of her superstructure and bridge and her machinery space differed from the two-compartment arrangement favoured in the British ships in having an extra compartment for the auxiliary diesel generators.

She could carry 690 first class and 736 second class passengers, and although she was employed mainly on day service, was provided with berths for 530 in dormitories and 12 private cabins.

She entered service in August 1950 under the management and colours of SAGA, but in May 1951 her funnel was repainted with SNCF's newly adopted buff with a black top.

She served continuously on the Calais-Folkestone service with only the occasional visit to Dover until 30 September 1972 when she was withdrawn and put up for sale pending the arrival of the new SNCF multi-purpose car ferry *Chartres*. In 1973 she was sold to the Monaco

Below: The elegant *Cote d'Azur* pictured in SAGA colours was the most powerful steamer ever built for the short sea route. Her white funnel was repainted buff in 1952. *Skyfotos*

based SA Monegasque d'Armement et de Navigation and appears to have been briefly renamed *Azur* however this had been changed to *Marie F* (Fondacci) by the time she arrived in Monaco on 8 July. Her new owners had intended a service to Sardinia and possibly Corsica and Italy starting that autumn but berthing arrangements at Monaco proved unsuitable and after an abortive plan to use her as a floating casino she was towed away to be laid up in the Etang de Berre near Marseilles.

She was sold for scrap in September to Jose Laborda Gonzales and was later towed to the small port of Murcia in Southern Spain where she was broken up in 1974.

Above: This view of her backing into Folkestone in September 1972 clearly shows the fine sheer of her hull and prominent knuckle forward. Note also the streamlined top of her bridge and thin Strombos type funnel. *Author*

Below: Another aerial view of her in later years with red funnel and dark blue hull. Following her sale to Monaco a white band was added below her black funnel top. *Skyfotos*

PART 4

Newhaven to Dieppe

Joint service: France 37/56ths   UK 19/56ths
divisions based on length of rail journey from ports to respective capitals
1862–1922 LBSCR
1923–1947 SR
1948–1962 British Transport Commission (Southern Region)
1963–1978 British Rail Board
1979–to date Sealink
      jointly with
1862–1908 Societe de Chemin de Fer de L'Ouest
1909–1935 Societe de Chemin de Fer de l'Etat
1936–to date Societe Nationale des Chemins de Fer

Brighton (1878), *Victoria*

These two steamers were specifically ordered by the LBSCR from John Elder & Co of Govan to cope with the increase in traffic expected to arise as a result of the Paris International Exhibition of 1878. Contracted to reach 15kts, the first ship, *Brighton*, reached 17.5kts in March of that year and a month later her sister ship *Victoria* averaged 17kts with her engines developing a mean indicated horse power figure of 1,763. Reported at the time to be the finest ships in Channel service they had the following main dimensions:

Length: 221ft 4in
Breadth: 27ft 8in
Depth/Draught: 10ft 6in/7ft 1.5in
Gross tonnage: 531/534

Machinery: Two-cylinder compound diagonal 48in, 83in x 60in stroke
Boilers: Four cylindrical Stroudley 80lb/sq in
Power: 2,000ihp
Speed: 15kts

Two funnelled ships, though these were not fully cased, their entry into service brought a number of innovations to the Newhaven-Dieppe run as they were the first ships to be built of steel; the first to employ steam steering gear

Below: An early photograph of *Brighton* **alongside the well known London & Paris hotel at Newhaven. Note her half-cased funnels.** *Author's Collection*

operated from the bridge; and the first to have fixed cylinder engines. Their original paddles were replaced by a new feathering type designed by William Stroudley, the Railway Company's renowned locomotive engineer, in 1880.

From the outset *Victoria* seemed destined to be the unluckier of the pair for she hit the pier at Newhaven on her maiden arrival and grounded near Rottingdean on her first crossing to Dieppe. On a foggy night on 13 April 1887 she stranded on rocks off Pointe d'Ailly due to an inoperative fog signal and in the ensuing panic one of her boats tipped up in the falls and 19 of its 21 occupants were drowned, these being the only fatalities ever suffered on this route. The ship herself was quickly broken apart by the sea.

Just two years later *Brighton*, again in fog, hit the pier whilst entering Dieppe and sank in the inner harbour. Sold 'as lies' to a French broker she was raised and repaired, later being resold to Pockett's Bristol Channel Steam Packet Company who employed her on excursion duties between Swansea, Ilfracombe and Lundy.

Requisitioned by the Admiralty during World War 1 she served as a minelayer in the Dardanelles and following the cessation of hostilities was sold to a Turkish company who continued to run her in local waters until she was scrapped in 1927 at the ripe old age of 49.

Above: A later view of *Brighton* after her sale to Pocketts for excursion work in the Bristol Channel, showing the addition of a bridge and new funnels. *Author's Collection*

Right: *Brighton* as an Admiralty water-carrier at Mudros during the Gallipoli campaign. Note that her funnels are once again only half-cased and her after saloon has been plated in. *Author's Collection*

Brittany (1882), Normandy

The LBSCR returned to John Elder, (later the Fairfield Shipbuilding & Engineering Co) for a further pair of paddle steamers in 1882. From the following table it can be seen that these were 10ft longer and faster than their immediate predecessors, their cost being just under £40,000 each.

Length: 231ft 0in
Breadth: 27ft 8in
Depth: 10ft 6in
Gross tonnage: 579/605
Machinery: Two-cylinder compound diagonal 46in, 83in x 60in stroke
Boilers: Four steel Stroudley 110lb/sq in
Power: 2,700ihp
Speed: 17kts

Better looking than *Brighton* and her sister ship because they had full length funnel casings, the main claim to fame of the new ships lay in the fact that they were the first to use the new feathering paddle floats which had been perfected in 1880 by William Stroudley, the Railway Company's renowned locomotive superintendent. Although these paddle floats were extremely complex and prone to breakdown their undoubted increase in efficiency and corresponding increase in speed brought them into overall use in a short space of time. Both ships recorded their fastest crossing times within a month of each other in the summer of 1885, *Brittany* taking 3hr 37min and *Normandy* 5min less.

In thick fog in June 1891 *Normandy* grounded on rocks near Beachy Head for several hours but refloated at high water, though damage received necessitated a trip to London for repairs. The following year *Brittany* was reboilered in Glasgow and the opportunity was taken to fit new taller funnels and to lengthen her superstructure from the after funnel to the mainmast.

In 1902 both ships were sold for £11,000 to Liverpool and Douglas Steamers who had started a service in opposition to the established Isle of Man Steam Packet Company. Their new owners failed however before they could enter service and they were sold for scrapping in the same year.

Above: *Normandy* lying in Newhaven during the latter stage of her LBSCR career showing the fine rake of her masts and funnels.
Laurence Dunn Collection

Left: A quarter view of *Brittany* alongside the East quay at Newhaven. Note her turtle back foc'sle.
Newhaven and Seaford Historical Society

Rouen, Paris (1888)

New steamers were required in view of the forthcoming Paris Exhibition in 1889 and *Rouen* and *Paris* duly appeared from the Fairfield yard at Govan in 1888. The last paddle steamers to be built for the LBSCR they were designed by Stroudley and were amongst the finest of their day. They shared the following dimensions:

Length: 250ft 6in
Breadth: 29ft 0in (55ft over paddleboxes)
Depth: 14ft 0in
Gross tonnage: 760
Machinery: Two-cylinder compound diagonal 46in, 83in x 72in stroke
Boilers: Four steel Stroudley 110lb/sq in
Power: 3,500ihp
Speed: 19kts (service)

Straight stemmed ships with two heavily raked funnels which were shorter and fatter than hitherto, in order to hide the steampipes, they could accommodate 706 passengers.

Although suffering from paddle problems they notched up some impressive times, the honours finally going to *Rouen* on 12 September 1888 with a passage of 3hr 20min corresponding to a speed of 19.2kts.

During a fierce storm early in 1890 whilst on passage from Dieppe some of *Paris*'s starboard paddle floats became loose and disabled she drifted some 60 miles up Channel. Off Cap Gris Nez the damaged floats fell off and restarting her engines she eventually reached Dover after a passage of some 36hr.

Rouen had problems of a different kind when she grounded in fog between Beachy and Seaford on 2 February 1897. However she refloated and reached Newhaven leaking badly. In 1903 she was sold to J. W. & R. P. Little of Barrow who renamed her *Duchess of Buccleuch* and ran her between that port and Douglas, Isle of Man for a further six years before disposing of her for scrap.

Bottom: Seen here in Dieppe the elegant *Paris* and her sister marked the highpoint of William Stroudley's marine designs. Her turtle back foc'sle was unusually long and note also the foresail which was used to steady the ship's head when entering port in stormy weather.
Author's Collection

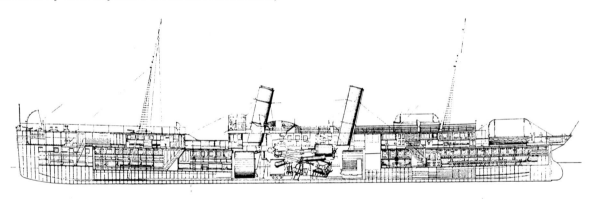

Paris remained with the railway company, though latterly in reserve, until the last month of 1912 when she was sold to the Shipping Federation. She was leased to the Admiralty for use as a minesweeper in March 1916 and was renamed *Verdun*. The suffix II was added to her name the following year and she was officially sold to her hirers.

She was repurchased by the Shipping Federation in April 1922 and was scrapped at Upnor on the Medway two years later, having outlived her sister-ship by some 15 years.

Left: An impressive view of *Paris* shortly after leaving the quay at Newhaven. *Newhaven and Seaford Historical Society*

Below: Following her sale *Rouen* became the *Duchess of Buccleuch*, pictured here approaching Douglas, Isle of Man. She has been fitted with a new flying bridge. *Author's Collection*

Seaford, Sussex

The LBSCR invited tenders early in 1893 for their first screw driven passenger steamer and William Denny of Dumbarton, thanks to their testing tank, were able to get nearest to the original specification of John Biles and won the order. Named *Seaford* after the town just to the East of Newhaven the new ship was launched on 19 April 1894. Her speed on trial in July was 20.16kts and her dimensions which had been modified slightly due to draught limitations at both the Sussex port and Dieppe were as follows:

Length (waterline): 268ft 9in (*Sussex* 275ft 0in)
Breadth: 34ft 1in
Depth/Draught: 14ft 6in/9ft 11in
Gross tonnage: 997 (*Sussex* 1,117)

Machinery: Two sets four-cylinder triple expansion
Boilers: Four SE tubular 160lb/sq in
Power: 5,000ihp
Speed: 20kts

She broke with tradition in having a single mast and funnel, the latter although raked being given a horizontal top which did not make for beauty. Accommodation was provided for 923 passengers, with berths for 82 in first and 64 in second class.

Her career was cut short, quite literally, when on 22 August 1895 she was rammed in fog in mid-Channel by the French railway cargo steamer *Lyon*. The blow fell on her port side between her two largest compartments and she foundered, but not before the *Lyon* had taken off all

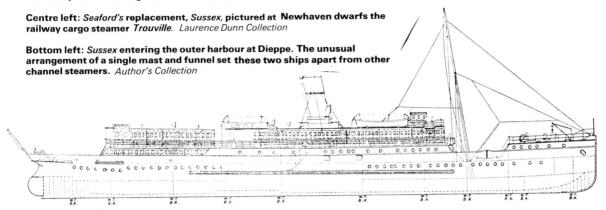

her passengers and crew. Seldom in the annals of cross-Channel history has a ship's life been so tragically short.

A replacement was ordered from Denny's almost immediately and took to the water as *Sussex* on 30 April the following year. She was tried in the Clyde in July reaching 20.4kts on the measured mile. Structurally she was virtually a repeat of *Seaford* but in the light of experience she was given slightly more length so as to include an extra watertight compartment.

Early in World War 1 she was taken over as a troopship but in February 1914 reverted to normal service but with a French crew. On 25 March 1916 whilst on passage from Folkestone to Dieppe her bows were blown off by a torpedo and she was later beached in the outer harbour at Boulogne. About 80 people lost their lives in the explosion, including all those in the first class saloon and also several Americans. The latter fact, following closely upon the *Lusitania* disaster is reported to have helped to persuade the United States to join the war.

Sussex was later salved and towed to Le Havre for rebuilding. Upon completion she was requisitioned by the French Navy who converted her to a minesweeper at Rochefort. After the war she was towed from Toulon to Genoa and was sold in 1920 to D. Demetriades, a Greek resident of Istanbul. Renamed *Aghia Sophia*, her career under the Greek flag was brief and she was reported as broken up in 1922/3.

Arundel, Brighton (1903)

Following three years successful operation with the *Sussex* Denny Bros were once again contracted by the LBSCR in July 1899 to build an improved version, which was to take no more than 3hr 12min for the crossing. The ship was launched at Dumbarton on 5 April 1900 and delivered on 24 June, her final cost being £68,070.

Named *Arundel* the new ship had the following main dimensions (*Brighton's* in brackets):

Length: 271ft 1in (273ft 1in)
Breadth: 34ft 0in (34ft 0in)
Depth/Draught: 14ft 6in/10ft 10in (11ft 9in)
Gross tonnage: 1,067 (1,129)
Machinery: Two sets four-cylinder triple expansion
(Three sets Parsons turbines one HP,
two LP driving three shafts)
Boilers: Two DE return tube
(Four SE tubular)
Power: 5,000ihp (6,000ihp estimated)
Speed (trial): 20.69kts (21.37kts)

As can be seen from the above she was very similar in size to *Sussex* but externally she was quite different having two funnels and masts and an upper deck which continued to the stern. She could carry about 800 passengers and of these 126 first class and 87 second class could be berthed.

Having noted the success of the world's first turbine passenger steamers on the Clyde the progressive LBSCR were quick to order their own example some two months ahead of the SER, although the latter's *The Queen* was delivered first and got the glory. The new ship was named *Brighton* and following her launch in June 1903 was handed over at Newhaven on 28 August. Resembling *Arundel* in appearance she proved to be slightly the faster of the two when both ran a comparative trial crossing to Dieppe and back on 27/28th, her average time being 3hr 3min, but more significantly her coal consumption was about 10% less. Lack of weight in her engine-room made her tender however compared with her sister and this was corrected by the addition of permanent concrete ballast.

On the morning of 6 November 1910, in poor visibility, *Brighton* was in collision with the world's largest full-rigged sailing ship, the 5,000ton steel five-master *Preussen* of the celebrated German Laesz

company. The latter's jib boom removed *Brighton*'s fore funnel and main mast and the impact also damaged lifeboats and deck fittings forcing her to return to Newhaven for extensive repairs. Meanwhile the *Preussen*, holed forward and minus her fore topmast, drifted up-Channel in deteriorating weather and eventually stranded near Dover to become a total loss. Fortunately no lives were lost in the incident.

During World War 1 *Arundel* served as a troopship as did *Brighton* initially, later becoming a hospital ship. The latter also carried the King to France and President Wilson and his wife to Calais and back from Dover.

Brighton was the first to be disposed of in October 1930 being somewhat surprisingly sold to Sir Walter Guiness (later Lord Moyne) for conversion to a private yacht. The work was carried out by Messrs Thornycroft at their Northam yard and she was given shorter funnels and an extended deckhouse. As great range was required she was converted to oil burning, her centre shaft was removed and she was given extra fuel tanks with a capacity of 500ton. During a subsequent refit in 1932 her turbines were replaced by two Polar Atlas diesel engines totalling 870bhp which gave her a speed of about 15kts, and one funnel was removed. Her career as a motorship was brief however as she hit a rock in fog off Galway in August 1933 and was wrecked.

Arundel lasted until February 1934 when she was sold to shipbreakers in Germany, her last years of employment having been mainly on cheap day excursions to France with a call at Brighton's Palace Pier en route.

Dieppe

Only two years after *Brighton*'s entry into service a second triple screw turbine ship joined the London & Brighton fleet, only this time she came from the Fairfield Company, the possible reason being that Denny's were already fully committed with orders for the SER. Launched on 6 April 1905 *Dieppe* recorded a speed of 21.64kts on a trial crossing and her dimensions, which were not dissimilar to *Brighton*, were as follows:

Length: 282ft 0in
Breadth: 34ft 8in

Depth/Draught: 14ft 6in/11ft 5in
Gross tonnage: 1,216 (later 1,228)
Machinery: Three sets Parsons turbines
(one HP, two LP)
Boilers: Four SE tubular 150lb/sq in
Power: 6,500ihp
Speed: 20kts

Outwardly she differed from the Denny ships in having shorter funnels and masts and a prominent and rather ugly spirket plate forward, also her superstructure

Above: A fine picture of *Dieppe* leaving Newhaven. The fact that *France* beyond is dressed overall and her speed is a little more than would normally be permitted in the harbour suggests that the occasion was her original trial crossing. *Author's Collection*

Right: A later view of *Dieppe* with a new navigating bridge and plated in promenade deck. *Author's Collection*

Below right: *Dieppe* is barely recognisable following her conversion to Lord Moyne's private motor yacht *Rosaura* as a replacement for the lost *Roussalka*. *Author's Collection*

bulwarks were plated. She was licensed to carry about 850 passengers (later 1,034).

During World War 1 she was used mainly for carrying troops, ammunition, and stores across the Channel, with a short period spent as a hospital ship. Sometime during the 1920s her superstructure was plated in during a winter refit but she was not converted to oil burning.

In September 1933 she was bought by Lord Moyne to replace the lost *Roussalka* (ex-*Brighton* (1903)). Renamed *Rosaura* she underwent a major £70,000 rebuild during the winter at Thornycroft's Woolston yard during which her turbines were replaced with two 1,150bhp Polar Atlas diesels, her centre shaft being removed, and she was given a new squat single funnel and a new bridge. Amongst her amenities were eight staterooms each with its own bathroom and a swimming pool on the weather deck. Her new speed was 15.5kts and she had a range of 15,000 miles, extra fuel tanks having been placed in her former boiler room.

Requisitioned at the beginning of World War 2 she saw service as an armed boarding vessel in the Mediterranean before being mined and sunk off Tobruk on 18 March 1941.

Paris (1913)

Following the entry into service of the new French turbine steamer *Newhaven*, the LBSCR ordered a new ship from Denny Bros in December 1911. After some delay they signified their agreement to the proposal of the shipbuilders and Messrs Parsons that she should be fitted with geared turbines, which had just been used with great success for the first time in the London & South Western's *Hantonia* and *Normannia*, though her oufit was to be considerably more powerful.

Paris was launched on 12 April 1913 and on her trials early in July attained a mean speed of 24.76kts which was then a record for her size of ship. Her main particulars were as follows:

Length: 301ft 0in
Breadth: 35ft 6in

Depth/Draught: 15ft 9in/11ft 5.5in
Gross tonnage: 1,774
Machinery: Four Parsons compound geared turbines
Boilers: Eight Yarrow w/t 202lb/sq in
Power: 15,000ihp
Speed: 24kts (contract)

On her arrival at Newhaven she made a trial trip to Dieppe on 14 July, returning the following day, her average speed being no less than 25.07kts. She could carry a total of 968 passengers and her accommodation was a great improvement on the earlier ships, berths being provided for first class in 16 single and 53 double cabins whilst second class had 128 in an open saloon. Exceptionally manoeuvrable she was the first London & Brighton ship to have a cruiser stern and as her lines had been modelled on destroyer principles she looked a real greyhound.

War broke out a year after her delivery and she was taken over by the Admiralty and converted into a minelayer for which her speed and shallow draught made her eminently suitable, though somewhat restricted by lack of range. She laid mines off the Belgian coast in 1916

Below: Paris **was probably making more than 25kts when this picture was taken during her speed trials in the Clyde. She was the first British Channel steamer to have a cruiser stern.** *Author's Collection*

and deep mines in the anti-submarine barriers in the Dover Strait, north of Scotland and off the Yorkshire coast in 1917/18. Returned to her owners, she resumed her normal peacetime service until the winter of 1928/9 when she was extensively refitted, emerging with a fully plated-in superstructure. In March 1932 her original boilers were replaced by four larger Yarrow ones which were oil-fired and from 1934 she took over from *Arundel* on the Tuesday and Thursday day excursions to Dieppe via Brighton Palace Pier.

Requisitioned in 1939 for the second time she was used as a troop carrier but the following January was converted to a hospital ship, later that year being the

Top: A wartime view of *Paris* as a minelayer. Note the addition of temporary screening aft and what appears to be a large searchlight. *IWM*

Above: *Paris* with enclosed promenade deck at the 1937 Royal Naval Review. *Laurence Dunn Collection*

only one to enter Calais during the evacuation. She made five trips to Dunkirk, rescuing 740 wounded on 29 May. On her sixth outward trip on 2 June she was bombed and immobilised, later sinking after further attacks about 10 miles off the beaches with the loss of 20 of her crew.

Worthing, Brighton (1933)

The *Worthing* was the first ship to be built for the Newhaven-Dieppe service by the SR which had absorbed the LBSCR in 1923. Denny's tender which offered the quickest building time was accepted and she continued the new styling introduced by the *Isle of Thanet* in 1925 though smaller and somewhat faster. Launched on 3 May 1928 she was delivered at Newhaven on 30 August having previously averaged 24.12kts on a return trial trip to Dieppe. As with other ships on that route she was only one-third British owned, the remaining two-thirds being held by France. She cost £172,000 and her main dimensions were:

Length (oa): 306ft 0in
Breadth: 38ft 6in
Depth/Draught: 15ft 9in/10ft 7in
Gross tonnage: 2,288/2,391
Machinery: Two sets Parsons single reduction geared turbines
Boilers: Four Yarrow oil-fired w/t 252lb/sq in closed stokehold
Power: 14,500/16,400ihp
Speed: 24kts

Worthing represented a major step forward from the *Paris*, her accommodation in particular being of a high standard and her total passenger capacity was 1,040 carried in three classes.

A similar ship but drawing slightly less water was ordered from Denny's in January 1932. Perpetuating the name *Brighton* she was launched on the last day of November, bad weather having prevented this happening after her christening the previous day. Following a successful trial to Dieppe and back during

Above: A fine view of *Worthing* at full speed during a crossing in August 1929. *A. M. S. Russell*

Left: *Worthing* as HMS *Brigadier* in her wartime role as an infantry landing ship. Her armament consisted of one 12-pounder and four 20mm anti-aircraft guns. *IWM*

Below left: *Brighton* dressed overall on the occasion of the Royal Naval Review on 20 May 1937. Note the large ventilators around her funnel.
Laurence Dunn Collection

which she averaged 24.69kts she was handed over to the Southern Railway on 22 March 1933. In looks she was to *Worthing* what *Canterbury* was to *Isle of Thanet*, as a result of her lifeboats being raised in order to provide more open deck space.

Both ships ran successfully until requisitioned early in 1939 for use as troop carriers along with *Paris*, subsequently becoming hospital ships. *Brighton* usually ran on her normal route carrying about 250 casualties at a time but she was caught at Dieppe by a heavy German air raid on 24 May 1940 and was sunk, happily without loss of life as her crew were ashore at the time.

Worthing made five trips to Dunkirk and in August that year was taken over by the Admiralty and renamed HMS *Brigadier*. She served as a Fleet Air Arm target ship for a while in 1941 and in 1942 was converted into an infantry landing ship carrying six LCAs. Her troop complement was 180 and she was armed with one 12-pounder and four 20mm anti-aircraft guns.

Above: This fine picture of *Brighton* meeting the south-westerly swell after clearing the outer breakwater at Newhaven shows clearly her different boat arrangement to that of *Worthing*. *Newhaven and Seaford Historical Society*

Returning to the Newhaven service on 24 March 1945 she saw a further ten years operation before being sold to John S. Latsis of Piraeus. Renamed *Phryne* she was given a white hull and commenced a weekly 17kt schedule from Piraeus to Samos, Paronaxias and Crete. Latsis thought that running her at this lower speed would be economical but this was not borne out in operation and after her class had been allowed to lapse in 1960 she was laid up and was eventually reported broken up in 1964.

Brighton (1950)

This much-favoured name was revived for the sixth time for the only postwar passenger steamer to be built for the English partners of the joint Newhaven-Dieppe service who since nationalisation in 1948 were now the British Transport Commission, Southern Region.

Brighton was launched by Denny's on 7 October 1949, leaving their yard for the first time towards the end of April the following year. Her turbines were of the single cylinder double casing impulse type, an innovation for Channel steamers. Her contract stipulated a speed of 24kts fully loaded and on the Skelmorlie mile she reached 24.5kts with her turbines producing 18,106shp.

Her main particulars were as follows:

Length (oa): 311ft 9in
Breadth: 40ft 6in
Depth/Draught: 16ft 9in/11ft 1in

Gross tonnage: 2,875
Machinery: Two sets Pametrada single
 reduction geared turbines
Boilers: Two Foster Wheeler oil-fired
 w/t 450lb/sq in
Power: 19,000shp (16,150shp astern)
Speed: 24kts

In looks she was quite different to the previous Newhaven ships being more in the same mould as *Maid of Orleans* completed by Denny's a year earlier. Her raked funnel was broad and squat and she was the first channel steamer to be fitted with tripod masts which required no rigging. Her accommodation included two berth cabins and open berths in two saloons for men and women and her total daytime capacity was 1,450. Her

turbines were of the single cylinder double casing impulse type, an innovation for Channel steamers.

Operating in conjunction with *Londres* and *Arromanches* and later *Lisieux* she continued on the mail service until the completion of the new car ferry terminal at Newhaven in June 1964. Thereafter her duties were relegated to relief work and no-passport excursions. She made a rare visit to Boulogne on a pilgrim excursion from Folkestone in July 1966 and was withdrawn following a final trip from Newhaven on 18 September on account of her excessive fuel consumption.

In December 1966 she was bought by Mr Cowasjee, the owner of Jersey Lines Ltd, who had previously taken *Sir Richard Grenville*, one of the railway owned Plymouth tenders, for a service between Jersey and Granville. She was renamed *La Duchesse de Bretagne* and proceeded to Antwerp for a three month refit during which she was fitted with two quarter ramps at upper deck level to permit the drive-on loading of about 20 cars. Alterations to her accommodation included the provision of aircraft type seating and a new bar.

On 15 May 1967 she sailed from Torquay at the start of an ambitious schedule of excursions which linked that

Above: Newhaven ships tended to be unique in looks and the powerful *Brighton* seen here on trials was no exception. She was the first Channel steamer with tripod masts and was undoubtedly one of the finest examples of Denny Bros shipbuilding expertise. *Laurence Dunn Collection*

port and Weymouth with the Channel Islands and St Malo, and by the end of the season on 25 September had carried just over 80,000 passengers and about 1,500 cars. The following year Southampton and Plymouth calls were instituted in place of Weymouth but this was to be her last season as her owner went bankrupt early in 1969 with debts totalling over half a million pounds. She was arrested in Southampton and was later sold to Messrs Pounds who towed her to a lay-up berth in Portsmouth harbour to await a buyer. None was forthcoming and she was sold for scrap in April 1970 being towed to Belgium where the Bruges Shipbreakers Co commenced work on 6 August.

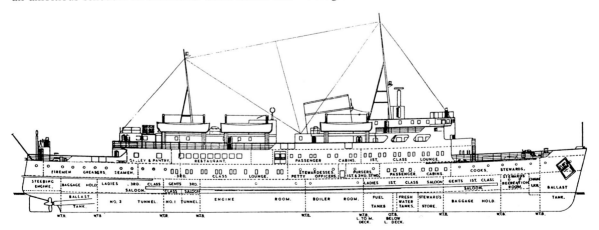

Her extravagant appetite for fuel had been one of the main causes of her owners' downfall and was probably the reason why she did not find favour with Greek buyers like her former running mates *Londres* and *Arromanches*. Nonetheless 20 years was rather a short life for a fine ship which was the last of her type built by the Denny yard at Dumbarton.

Above: A Solent view of *Brighton* **as** *La Duchesse de Bretagne* **taken in June 1968 following her sale to Jersey Lines Ltd. Note the alterations aft to allow cars to be driven on by means of hinged ramps. Her new colours were maroon funnel and dark blue hull.** *Author*

Seine, Tamise, Manche

Back in 1851 at the start of the joint Anglo/French service between Newhaven and Dieppe the French partners Le Chemin de Fer de L'Ouest had provided two-thirds of the capital because Paris was roughly twice as far from the Channel as London. At first all ships although jointly owned in like proportion were British-built and manned but in 1887 four cargo steamers were transferred to the French flag. Shortly afterwards the French decided to build their first passenger ship stipulating that in future two-thirds of the passenger fleet should be French-manned. In view of the original capital outlay the LBSCR could not argue though their acceptance was no doubt due in part to the influence of

Sir Edward Blount, the dominant chairman of the French Company.

The new ship was built at the Le Havre yard of the Forges et Chantiers de la Mediterranee which was to become the French equivalent of Denny Bros producing all the subsequent French Channel steamers. Christened *Seine* she was delivered early in August 1891.

Her main particulars were:

Length: 269ft 0in
Breadth: 29ft 6in
Depth/Draught: 15ft 6in (ors 15ft 2in)
Gross tonnage: 808 (ors 978)

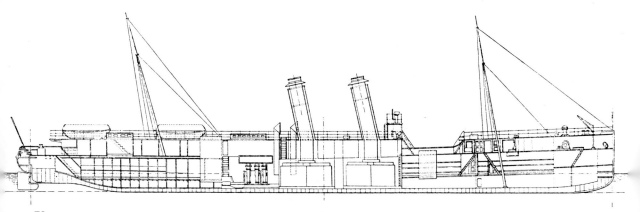

Left: The 1891-built *Seine* was the first French-built Channel passenger steamer and she introduced a new profile which included one of the earliest cruiser sterns.
Newhaven and Seaford Historical Society

Below: *Tamise* differed from *Seine* in having shorter funnels of slightly greater diameter, more ventilators, and an extended upper deck. Folding canvas screens were used to protect the promenade deck during bad weather.
Laurence Dunn Collection

Bottom: *Manche* pictured arriving at Newhaven could be distinguished from the very similar *Tamise* by her large brass whistle on the forward funnel.
Author's Collection

Machinery: Two sets six cylinder triple expansion
Boilers: Seine 6 cylindrical r/t 156lb/sq in
others 12 Belleville w/t 242lb/sq in
Power: 4,000ihp (ors 4,500ihp)
Speed: 19.2kts (contract)

Above: A rare view of Manche in later life as Le Verdon in Bordeaux. Note the narrower black tops to her funnels and provision of awnings, also extra boats aft.
Author's Collection

Introducing an entirely new and not unpleasing profile to the Channel the twin funnelled *Seine* was received with acclaim because she was faster than the British paddlers, her first crossing on 8 August 1891 taking only 3hr 11min, and she also burned about a ton less fuel per crossing. In many ways she was an innovative ship for the time, being the first cross-Channel passenger ship to have a cruiser stern and the first to employ water tube boilers. However her builders lacked the experience of the British shipyards and her speed was obtained by the adoption of a narrow beam and somewhat light construction. These gave her a propensity to roll and she did not stand up well to the rigours of service necessitating costly repairs.

An improved and more strongly built sister ship named *Tamise* (Thames) appeared in November 1893, her first crossing taking 3hr 3min, equal to a speed of 21kts. Lit throughout by electricity she could carry around 750 passengers. Draught problems were eased by the adoption of the new lightweight Belleville water tube boilers though these were not without their teething troubles, not the least being the consumption of about four tons more coal per trip than the earlier ship.

In December 1892 *Seine* had lost a propeller and broken a tailshaft after contacting the chains of the Newhaven dredger and in 1896 British efforts to have her

sold were unsuccessful. However the French agreed to build a new ship and on 1 April 1897 launched the *Manche* (Channel), a near identical sister to *Tamise* but with improved accommodation. Her maiden crossing of a fraction of a minute under 3hr was the fastest yet.

Seine having failed to attract a buyer following damage incurred in March 1898 was used for possibly the last time during the Paris Exhibition of 1900. She was permanently laid up on 2 March 1901 and was sold to a Brest scrap dealer in December 1905.

Tamise and *Manche* continued in service until replaced by the new French turbine steamers in 1911, the former being laid up on 3 June 1912 and the latter on 2 December. Negotiations for their sale to Turkish principals fell through due to the outbreak of war in the Balkans and *Tamise* was sold early in 1914 to a Dunkirk scrap dealer though she was not towed there until after World War 1. At the same time *Manche* went south to become the Bordeaux Chamber of Commerce's *Le Vedun*. She maintained a ferry service to Royan at the mouth of the Geronde until eventually broken up in 1919.

The novelty of these three ships represented a bold decision on the part of their builder and did much to enhance the reputation of French shipyards in general.

France

With *Seine* proving to be rather unsatisfactory and no doubt with the 1900 Paris International Exhibition in mind a fourth French steamer was ordered from the F. & C. de la Mediterranee in August 1898. She was given the name *France* at her launching on 8 June 1899 and made

her official trial crossings to Newhaven and back at the end of August, her average time in poor conditions being 3hr 28sec.

She was slightly smaller than the previous ships as the following table of her dimensions shows:

Left: *France* leaving the inner harbour at Dieppe following a refit. She could easily be recognised from her consorts by her ugly, upright funnels.
Author's Collection

Below: *France* at a later stage with a wheelhouse and her turtle-back foc'sle extended to the superstructure. The flag signals denote the number of passengers she is carrying in each class so that a train of appropriate size could be made up whilst she was docking.
Author's Collection

Length: 264ft 0in
Breadth: 29ft 5in
Depth: 15ft 1in
Gross tonnage: 729
Machinery: Two six cylinder triple expansion reciprocating
Boilers: 12 Belleville w/t 242lb/sq in
Power: 4,500ihp
Speed: 19.2kts

Although similar in dimension to her predecessors she differed considerably from them in looks through having two thin, upright funnels without the spark arrester tops and her masts were also without rake. Other differences included improved accommodation and a different system of engine room ventilation which employed louvres in her funnel houses instead of the earlier prominent cowl ventilators. The latter was clearly not very satisfactory for she suffered from overheating problems from the outset.

On 1 March 1900 she suffered an explosion in her engine room which killed nine stokers and seriously injured two more. The cause was traced to her copper tubing which had proved unequal to the high pressures being developed and it was replaced with steel tubes in a four month refit.

During the course of a further refit in the first half of 1905 her hull was strengthened and improvements were carried out to her second class accommodation whilst provision was made for the carriage of third class passengers aft. The gap between her foc'sle and superstructure was plated in to provide a new second class smoking room and this resulted in her gross tonnage being increased to 944.

Newhaven, Rouen (1912)

With the turbine firmly established on the Newhaven-Dieppe run in the shape of the British built *Brighton* and *Dieppe* the Western Railway of France stipulated this form of propulsion for two new steamers to replace *Tamise, Manche* and *France. Newhaven* and *Rouen* (originally to be called *London*) were delivered by the F. & C. de la Mediterrannee in May 1911 and September 1912 at a price of around £87,500 each. They marked a considerable step forward in design and size from the previous ships and had the following main particulars:

Length: 301ft 9in
Breadth: 34ft 7in
Depth/Draught: 14ft 6in/11ft 6in
Gross tonnage: 1,546
Machinery: Three direct coupled Parsons turbines
(one HP, two LP)
Boilers: Four w/t
Power: 10,000ihp
Speed: 21.75kts (contract)

Fine looking ships with two tall slightly raked funnels and short masts they quickly showed their superiority in speed, *Newhaven* averaging 23.85kts on her official

Whilst inward bound to Newhaven on 5 November 1911 she was struck by a heavy sea and broached. In trying to avoid the outer breakwater she touched bottom and broke her rudder but by steering with her engines managed to regain the open sea and was later towed in by the local tug *Albert.*

In November 1913 she was sold to the Riviera based Tourisme Nautique SA who gave her a white hull and yellow funnels and employed her without change of name as a 'cruising yacht' between Cannes, Nice, Monaco, Menton and Genoa. The onset of war in 1914 brought this brief phase in her career to a close and she was later repurchased by her original owners and chartered to the Admiralty in July 1915 for use as a cross-Channel troop transport. Released in April 1919 she was refitted and returned to the Newhaven run on 4th November but was laid up shortly afterward following the breakdown of her starboard propeller shaft.

On 21 October 1920 she was sold to an Argentine buyer C. Seguin who renamed her *Fortuna* and converted her to a pleasure steamer. She left Dieppe bound for South America on 21 December 1921 but met with difficulties in the Atlantic and was towed back to Lorient. She eventually reached Buenos Aires and took up her new duty carrying gamblers to the casino town of Mar del Plata.

She changed hands in 1931, her owners being the Montevideo based Comp Argentina Uruguaya de Nav Centenario who named her *Centenario* and presumably placed on the Montevideo-Buenos Aires run. Although she remained in the Register until 1962 she is believed to have been wrecked some time before this date.

return trial trip on 26/27 May which was 17min better than the time of 3hr stipulated in the contract. *Rouen* bettered this by achieving 24.06kts the following September. Both ships were highly manoeuvrable, the change over from ahead to astern taking only four seconds and they could be stopped in their own length from a little over 12kts. Their passenger capacity was about 1,000 people.

Following the outbreak of war in 1914 both were requisitioned by the French navy for use as auxiliary scouts with the 2nd Light Squadron, Channel and whilst

Top right: The turbine driven *Rouen* leaving Newhaven early in her career. Note the tall funnels and short masts, also her open bridge. *Laurence Dunn Collection*

Centre right: An impressive view of *Newhaven* as a hospital ship during World War 1. The funnels of both ships had been shortened before the war and they were given higher bridges after the war. *Author's Collection*

Right: *Rouen* looking very different with a single large funnel and plated in superstructure following her 1932 refit. Note also that her mainmast has been moved forward. *A. R. Tetreau Collection*

acting in this capacity *Rouen* was torpedoed on 29 December 1916 by a German submarine whilst returning from a sortie in the Bay of St Malo, losing her bow forward of the bridge and five of her crew killed. She drifted up Channel but was towed into Cherbourg and repaired. Subsequently she served for a while as a seaplane carrier before proceeding in 1917 to the Mediterranean on trooping duty between Taranto and Corfu/Itea. In the meantime her sister had been transferred to the Admiralty for hospital service between Scapa Flow and the south, later acting as a troopship. She returned to peacetime service on 5 July 1920 some 11 months after *Rouen*.

On 5 August 1924 *Newhaven* stranded under the cliffs of Berneval near Dieppe, in foggy weather. Damage was slight and she was towed off on 14th and repaired.

Both ships underwent extensive refits during the winter of 1929/30 emerging with improved accommodation and enclosed promenade decks which increased their gross measurement by 300ton. In March 1932 *Rouen* was converted to burn oil-fuel and was given a new and larger single funnel, her sister being treated likewise in September of the following year. These measures were considered to be cheaper than ordering new tonnage in the unhappy economic climate prevailing at the time.

In 1940 they were requisitioned once again to carry troops to Dunkirk later helping to evacuate them together with many refugees. Whilst following the evacuation westwards around the French coast *Newhaven* was seized by the German navy at Rochefort on 26 July 1940 and *Rouen*, after running short of fuel whilst trying to reach England, at Le Verdon on 30 August. *Newhaven* became the auxiliary patrol vessel *Skorpion* in 1943 and later in turn the depot ship *Skagerrack* and the accommodation ship *Barbara*. *Rouen* served first as the auxiliary cruiser *Natter* in 1941 and the following year became the experimental ship *Wullenwever*, suffering mine damage in the Baltic on 25 April 1943.

After the war both ships were returned to Dieppe from Kiel in October 1945. They were towed to Le Treport in August 1946 and lay there for three years until towed away for scrapping, *Newhaven* going to Ghent and *Rouen* to Dieppe. Their respective careers of 38 and 39 years had certainly been full of variety.

Versailles

A further fast passenger steamer for the French partners of the Joint Newhaven Service was put in hand by the Forges & Chantiers de la Mediterranee in 1914, however war intervened and all work on her was suspended. After the war construction resumed only slowly at first due to the austerity conditions prevailing at the time and she was not finally completed until July 1921.

Named *Versailles*, in commemoration of the peace treaty which had ended the war, she was some 200ton larger than the Denny-built *Paris* and her main particulars were as follows:

Length: 305ft 6in
Breadth: 36ft 2in

Depth/Draught: 15ft 7in/9ft 10in
Gross tonnage: 1,971
Machinery: Two sets Parsons single reduction geared turbines
Boilers: Eight w/t Delaunay-Belleville 256lb/sq in
Power: 15,000ihp
Speed: 24kts (service)

Below: Versailles at speed in the Channel before her funnels were repainted yellow after 1923. Note her prominent wood-sheathed bridge. *Author's Collection*

Designwise she closely resembled *Newhaven* and *Rouen* as they looked after their funnels had been shortened and bridges raised but she could always be distinguished from them by having three pairs of boats. Her turbine machinery was built by the shipbuilders and was designed to give her a maximum speed of about 25kts at full power. During her official trial crossing from Dieppe on 1 August 1921 in rather rough conditions she averaged 24.37kts, raising this to 24.83kts on her return the following day in more moderate seas.

In 1929 her stokehold was converted to oil-firing and during a further refit early in 1933 her promenade deck was plated in. Shortly after this she touched bottom in the trough of a large wave whilst leaving Newhaven and badly damaged her rudder. She managed to manoeuvre herself to shelter in the lea of Beachy Head and was later towed back by the tug *Foremost*.

Her history during the early part of World War 2 was

similar to that of her French built predecessors but she was damaged at Dunkirk and taken to Brest for layup, later being towed to Nantes where she was seized by the Germans. Paid off in 1942 she became an accommodation ship and at the end of hostilities was lying damaged at the Danish port of Aalborg. Although returned to France she was not considered worth repairing and was scrapped.

Londres, Arromanches

Just before the start of World War 2, the Chemin de Fer de L'Ouest and the Southern Railway had jointly placed an order with the F. and C. de la Mediterranee for a pair of twin-screw turbine passenger ships to replace *Newhaven* and *Rouen*. Their provisional names were *Dieppe* and *Newhaven* but during the Vichy period these were changed to *Londres* and *Vichy*. *Londres* was seized on the stocks when the Germans arrived in Le Havre but was launched on 19 December 1941 and after much delay was taken to Germany in 1943 for completion as the minelayer *Lothringen*. She was used in the Elbe and Weser Estuaries and later saw service in Denmark.

Returned from Kiel to her builders in 1945, she was refitted and entered her intended service on 18 April 1947. Her sister, renamed *Arromanches* to commemorate the Normandy invasion beach, was eventually launched in March 1946 and entered service the following summer. The main characteristics of both ships were as follows:

Length: 308ft 5in
Breadth: 42ft 4in
Depth/Draught: 23ft 4in/10ft 9in
Gross tonnage: 2,434/2,600
Machinery: Two sets Parsons SR geared turbines
Boilers: Two oil-fired superheated w/t by Penhoet
Power: 22,000shp (12,000shp astern)
Speed: 24kts

Straight stemmed ships with riveted hulls, they had three full length decks, with a boat-deck and short bridge deck. A single squarish raking funnel and two raking masts completed an impression of restrained power, for they were without question the most powerful Channel ships yet built. Their full passenger complement of 1,450 persons, roughly the equivalent of a full train, were carried in first and third classes, and they had 14 private cabins. Berths numbered 402.

In May 1955 the British Transport Commission, having sold *Worthing*, took over the ownership of *Londres*, and gave her an English crew. She continued

Below: The powerful *Londres* at Newhaven in April 1947. Note her surprisingly old-fashioned vertical stem and the large air intakes in her funnel. *Laurence Dunn Collection*

Right: Spotless and dressed overall, *Arromanches* speeds the President of France towards Dover at the start of a State visit in March 1950. Her boats have been raised in their davits to provide more deck space. *Skyfotos*

Below right: *Londres* as the Typaldos inter-island steamer, *Sofoklis Venizelos* with soft-nosed raking stem and single streamlined mast. *Author's Collection*

until the end of 1963 when she was put up for sale due to the impending opening of the new car ferry service. Bought by Typaldos Bros in December, she made her way out to Greece under the name of *Ionion II*. Following alteration, which included the addition of a new raked stem, and a new stream-lined foremast, and the removal of her mainmast, she was renamed *Sophoklis Venizelos* and was placed in service carrying passengers and cars from Piraeus to the Islands, usually Crete or Rhodes. Whilst refitting in April 1966 she caught fire on the 14th, and was towed out of harbour and beached the following day. She was not repaired and was eventually broken up.

Arromanches remained in service until 1964, grounding just east of Newhaven Harbour on the 8 July in severe weather, but she refloated without damage. Replaced by *Falaise* which had inaugurated the new car ferry service, she was sold in 1965 to Petros Nomikos Ltd of Piraeus (a relative newcomer to the Greek passenger

scene) and ran under the name of *Leto* between Piraeus and the islands of Tenos and Mykonos on the daily 'Cyklades Express' service.

On 25 October 1970 she struck bottom whilst leaving Tenos Harbour in a gale and damaged her rudder and port propeller. She was driven out of control to the nearby island of Syros and was towed in by two tugs the following day. She was eventually broken up by Atlantis Dialissi Plion at Eleusis between December 1972 and July 1973.

Lisieux

In 1951 French Railways returned to the F. & C. de la Mediterranee with an order for what was destined to become their last cross-Channel passenger vessel to be built at the Le Havre yard. Named *Lisieux* she was launched on 26 February 1952, undergoing her trials later that year during which she averaged 25.4kts, the fastest speed yet achieved.

Bearing a strong resemblance to the same builder's *Cote d'Azur* (qv) which had appeared on the Folkestone/ Calais route in 1951, she was however appreciably smaller as the following table of dimensions shows:

Length: 313ft 4in
Breadth: 42ft 8in
Depth/Draught: 33ft 3in/10ft 6in
Gross tonnage: 2,946
Machinery: Two sets Parsons SR geared turbines
Boilers: Two oil-fired w/t FCM 47/60 426lb/sq in
Power: 22,000shp
Speed: 24kts (22.5kts in service on one boiler)

A five deck ship, two of which were continuous, her hull was sub-divided by 10 watertight bulkheads and much use was made of light alloy in her superstructure. Her streamlined bridge echoed that of *Cote d'Azur* as did her Strombos type funnel, and her passenger complement was about 1,450. Her engines were the same as the other ship but her boilers were of a new type which allowed more rapid firing and easier power variation. Her entry into service in 1953 displaced the *Worthing* and *Londres* was transferred to the British Flag, thus giving two ships from each country on the run.

Owing to a reduction in passenger traffic her winter service was suspended from October 1958 and henceforth she only operated from March to October. Although the new car ferry service was now in operation, she started the summer season with *Brighton* in 1965, but so few passengers were carried that she was withdrawn in June, making her last sailing from Newhaven on the 26th of that month. For the remainder of the season she was somewhat unusually chartered by the Compagnie

Generale Transatlantique for a 12-week period, her service being a five-day weekly one between St Malo and Jersey, but with day excursions to Guernsey from Torquay on Wednesdays and a sailing from Weymouth on Thursday nights.

The service incurred heavy losses and she was laid up over the winter, being sold the following February to Petros Nomikos for about £267,000. After refitting at Le Havre she left for Piraeus in April renamed *Apollon* with a white painted hull and a month later she commenced running between Piraeus and the Cyclades Islands. Nomikos ships had a good reputation for efficiency and were used by the knowledgeable.

In 1976 Nomikos withdrew from the passenger business and *Apollon* was sold to Agapitos Bros, another Piraeus-based company, who continue to run her at the time of writing, her service being a daily year-round one to Tinos and Mykonos. The only surviving example of a French built cross-Channel passenger vessel, her days must surely be numbered as the ubiquitous car ferry is fast taking over on the Greek inter-island services.

Below: *Lisieux* **leaves the white cliffs of Beachy Head behind as she speeds on her way towards Dieppe. Note her streamlined bridge and narrow aerofoil type funnel.** *Skyfotos*

Bottom: A 1977 view of *Lisieux* **as the Greek Agapitos steamer** *Apollon* **passing between the island of Fleves and the mainland on her daily run to the Cyclades. Her white funnel has a green top and design and her promenade deck has been extended to the stern.** *Author*

1862–1922 LSWR
1923–1947 SR
1948–1962 British Transport Commission (Southern Region)
1963–1978 British Rail Board
1979–to date Sealink UK

Ella, Hilda

The LSWR were amongst the first of the cross-Channel operators to abandon paddle propulsion in favour of the screw. By 1880 they owned several such vessels, the most recent being the *Diana* built at the Whiteinch yard of Aitken & Mansel, Glasgow in 1876. It was to the same yard that the railway company returned for a pair of larger and improved 'Diana's' some five years later. These emerged in 1881 and 1882 as *Ella* and *Hilda*, their costs being £28,850 and £33,000 respectively and their main particulars were as follows:

Length: 235ft 5in
Breadth: 29ft 1in
Depth: 14ft 2in
Gross tonnage: 820
Machinery: Single two-cylinder compound by
        J. & J. Thomson
Boilers: 85lb/sq in
Power: 1,333ihp
Speed: 13.5kts

They were single deck steamers built of iron with a straight stem, foc'sle, and long poop leading to a rather square counter stern. Two tall, closely spaced masts and a single funnel gave them a yacht-like appearance and they could carry about 580 passengers. *Ella* normally ran on the Cherbourg service whilst *Hilda* maintained the Southampton-Channel Islands and St Malo run.

In 1893 *Hilda* was reboilered and fitted with electric light by Messrs Day & Summers, Southampton who dealt similarly with *Ella* during the winter of 1896/7.

On the night of 18 November 1905 after 23 years in service *Hilda* struck the Rocher du Jardin whilst entering St Malo in a blizzard and broke her back and foundered with the loss of 128 lives. Her sister remained with the railway company until the end of July 1913 when she was sold to the Shipping Federation for £4,500 and left Southampton for Liverpool. Her subsequent career is shrouded in mystery but she was finally broken up in 1926/7.

Below: *Ella* **and her sister were amongst the earliest examples of screw-driven Channel steamers. The LSWR's colours were a black hull with a white band and a buff funnel.** *Author's Collection*

Laura

The next steamer to enter the fleet of the LSWR was the *Laura* which was delivered by Aitken & Mansel in 1885. She replaced the old paddle steamer *Caesarea*, which had been sunk the previous year, on the Southampton-Channel Islands and St Malo service. A smaller vessel than her immediate predecessors though similar in appearance, she was the first of the company's ships to be built of steel and she cost £23,500.

Her main dimensions were:

Length: 207ft 3in
Breadth: 26ft 8in
Depth: 13ft 3in
Gross tonnage: 641
Machinery: Two-cylinder compound
Boilers: Two cylindrical
Power: 1,169ihp
Speed: 13kts

Not long after entering service on 26 January 1886 the bottom of her high pressure cylinder blew out, killing a coal trimmer and necessitating her being towed to Guernsey and thence to Southampton for repairs.

After the introduction of newer and faster ships she appears to have become more associated with some of the smaller ports in the Bay of St Malo such as Granville and early in 1922 she was downgraded to a cargo carrier. On 7 November 1925 she fractured her rudder in mid Channel whilst bound for St Malo and was towed back to Southampton by the British steamer *Magic Star*.

Below: *Laura* in the early 1920s shortly before she became a cargo ship. *Author's Collection*

After 42 years useful service, the last four under Southern Railway flag, she was sold in October 1927 to the Bahamas Shipping Company, Nassau and following a short refit on the Clyde left on what has been reported as a 'nightmare' delivery voyage across the Atlantic to Miami, almost running out of fuel en route.

The following year she changed hands again, being sold locally to the Florida Inter-Islands SS Co Ltd who

Above: The diminutive *Laura* **at Granville. She could be told apart from the earlier ships by her thinner funnel and raised boats aft.** *Author's Collection*

renamed her *City of Nassau*. Some reports place her as being later wrecked whilst carrying 'bootleg' spirits during prohibition but the Register records her as having been broken up in 1937.

Dora

In May 1888 the LSWR invited tenders from six companies for a new steamer of 15/16kts speed. The lowest bid of £32,800 for a 16-knot ship came from Robert Napier & Sons, Glasgow, and was accepted thus breaking the Company's links with Aitken & Mansel.

The new ship was launched on 2 March 1889 and underwent trials in Stokes Bay on 30 April. She was the largest yet built for the railway company and her main particulars were as follows:

Length: 240ft 0in
Breadth: 30ft 0in
Depth: 14ft 3in
Gross tonnage: 813

Right: An early view of *Dora* **in her original LSWR colours.**
Author's Collection

Machinery: Triple expansion
Boilers: Two DE tubular 160lb/sq in
Power: 2,250ihp
Speed: 16kts (contract)

Representing a logical development in design from the previous ships the side of her superstructure was plated in and her mainmast was placed further aft. She was the first ship in the company to be electrically lit and the first to adopt triple expansion propulsion, her power being increased a year after delivery by the provision of a forced draught system. Sleeping accommodation was provided for 140 passengers in first class and 60 second class passengers.

On 17 September 1892 she struck the Tasse Rock off Guernsey, repairs taking a month, and on 16 May the following year she hit again off Guernsey and was towed to St Peter Port by the Great Western steamer *Lynx*. A

noted roller she was not popular with the travelling public and was sold to the Isle of Man Steam Packet Company on 26 July 1901 after only 12 years service.

Renamed *Douglas* she was placed on the Liverpool-Douglas run and on 6 November 1903 she collided with and sank the steamer *City of Lisbon* in the Mersey. Some 20 years later having operated mainly on the night service she herself was sunk in collision with the *Artemisia* off Herculaneum Dock on 16 August 1923, happily without loss of life.

Frederica, Lydia, Stella

In September 1889 following the entry into service of the three new GWR steamers the LSWR decided to order three 17kt twin-screw ships in retaliation, the builders chosen being Messrs J. & G. Thomson of Clydebank who produced the lowest of the three bids received. *Vera, Lydia* and *Clara* were discussed as potential names but these were later altered to *Frederica, Lydia* and *Stella*, the first named undergoing trials in Stokes Bay on 21-22 July 1890 during which she comfortably exceeded her contract speed by obtaining 18.79kts under normal draught and 19.46kts with forced draught.

Similar speeds were reached by the other two ships which followed in September and October respectively and all three shared the following main particulars:

Length: 253ft 0in
Breadth: 35ft 1in
Depth: 14ft 8in
Gross tonnage: 1,059
Machinery: Two sets three-cylinder triple expansion
Boilers: Two DE cylindrical 160lb/sq in
Power: 5,700ihp
Speed: 17kts (contract minimum)

The first ships in the company to exceed 1,000ton they were extremely handsome and represented the final stage of evolution of the yacht-like design produced by Professor Biles, the consultant naval architect. Ten months after entering service *Lydia* hit a rock off

Guernsey and was out of commission for two weeks and on 1 December 1903 *Frederica* was transferred to the Southampton-Le Havre route in place of the older paddle steamers, later having the distinction of carrying the Company directors at the Jubilee Naval Review in June 1897.

Stella's career came to an untimely end just after 4.00pm on 30 March 1899 when she struck Black Rock off the Casquets and foundered with the loss of 105 lives. The same company's *Vera* and GWR's *Lynx* between them saved 119 people. This disaster was instrumental in bringing about an end to racing between the two railway companies who henceforth agreed to pool their services.

Due to her poor state of repair the LSWR considered selling *Lydia* in 1898 then decided otherwise and she was refitted and reboilered, the work being undertaken over a period of four and a half months by Messrs Day and Summers in Southampton at a cost of £6,500. *Frederica* underwent similar treatment during a 1904 refit and her funnel was lengthened at the same time. In June 1911 she was sold to Idarei Massousieh of Constantinople through the intervention of the Turkish Shipping Commission and was renamed *Nilufer*. The following year her ownership was changed to the Administration de Navigation a Vapeur Ottomane and she eventually became a war loss, being mined off Schili at the entrance to the Bosphorus on 22 November 1914.

Lydia survived World War 2 and was sold for £20,000 in December 1919 to an intermediary who resold her a year later to Coast Lines Ltd. She ran for them for a couple of years between Preston and Dublin before being sold for a third time to Greece where she was renamed *Ierax* and joined one of her old Great Western rivals, *Antelope*, in the Yannoulatos owned Ionian Steamship Company fleet. This company was absorbed into the newly formed Hellenic Coast Lines Co Ltd in 1929 and *Ierax* was scrapped in Italy in the autumn of 1933.

Alma, Columbia

Early in 1894 the LSWR invited bids for two new steamers for their Le Havre service and once again J. & G. Thomson were successful in obtaining the contract with a price of £50,000 per vessel. Construction took only six months and *Columbia* was delivered in Southampton on 19 October 1894 followed by her sister in December, their entry into service releasing the *Frederica*.

Their main particulars were:

Length: 270ft 7in
Breadth: 34ft 0in
Depth: 14ft 6in
Gross tonnage: 1,145

Machinery: Two sets four cylinder triple expansion
Boilers: Two vertical Serve type tubular
Power: 3,300ihp (60lb/sq in)
Speed: 19kts (contract)

Quite unlike any previous LSWR ships they had solid looking, flush hulls with a long deckhouse topped by two widely spaced funnels. They were designed specifically for overnight service to fit in with the Compagnie Generale Transatlantique's sailings from Le Havre and to this end were fitted with separate twin berth cabins for first class passengers, being pioneers in this respect. Total passenger capacity was about 153 in berths.

Left: *Alma* was the first twin-funnelled ship built for the LSWR for almost 30 years and she and her sister introduced new standards of comfort. *Laurence Dunn Collection*

Alma had a minor collision in fog with the four-masted sailing ship *Kate Thomas* on 21 March 1895 and *Columbia* contacted the steamer *Vesuvi* off Calshot on the morning of 17 February 1897, damage in both cases being slight. Later the same year *Columbia* was present at the Spithead Jubilee Review.

Both ships were subsequently reboilered, *Columbia* in 1906 when her funnels were moved closer together, and *Alma* without alteration the following year.

Columbia was sold on 16 April 1912 to an Algerian, Juan Sitges who renamed her *Sitges* and placed her under the Spanish flag. In 1915 she was purchased by the French navy and converted to the auxiliary cruiser *Corse* but was torpedoed and sunk off La Ciotat on 24 January 1918.

Alma had been disposed of three weeks after her sister to E. A. Cohan and made her way out east being re-

Above: *Columbia* **viewed from the same angle with a new funnel arrangement following her 1906 refit.** *Author's Collection*

registered the following year in the name of the Eastern Shipping Co Ltd of Penang. Towards 1917 she was briefly in the hands of P. N. F. Heath before passing to Japanese owners M. Matsou and U. Matsumoto of Nagasaki who renamed her *Shokiku Maru No2* (later *Shogiku Maru No2*). She was sold yet again in the early 1920s to Hongo Ikichiro of Amiro and was finally wrecked west of Sakhalin Island on 17 June 1924.

During their 18 years on the Channel both ships had done much to enhance the reputation of the Le Havre service and *Alma*'s subsequent travels must be something of a record for a Channel steamer.

Victoria (1896)

Plans for a new steamer for the Jersey-Granville/St Malo service were submitted in February 1896, the order again going to Messrs J. & G. Thomson. Named *Victoria* at her launch on 15 June the same year she carried out trials on

15 July and arrived in Southampton three days later. A smaller version of *Alma* and *Columbia* which she resembled in appearance, she had the following main dimensions:

Right: *Victoria* **shown leaving St Helier was basically a smaller version of** *Alma* **and** *Columbia* **but had a different boat arrangement.** *Author's Collection*

Length: 220ft 5in
Breadth: 28ft 1in
Depth: 16ft 3in
Gross tonnage: 709
Machinery: Two sets three-cylinder triple expansion
Boilers: Two SE cylindrical
Power: 1,500ihp
Speed: 16.5kts

She made her maiden voyage out to Jersey on 25 July and was a great improvement on the old paddle steamer *Alliance* which had operated the Jersey-France service previously. At some stage she had an extra pair of large lifeboats added to her long afterdeck which made her more readily distinguishable from the two Le Havre ships.

She was later transferred to Plymouth where she acted as a tender for the many liners which called in there to drop passengers for onward carriage by rail to London.

In June 1919 she was sold to the James Dredging, Towing & Transport Co Ltd who used her as an accommodation ship for workmen in Southampton for about six years after which she passed to the Greek Patriotic Cie de Nav Vapeur et d'Armement, under the management of K. Kallias and L. Teryazos, of Piraeus. The Teryazos family seem to have become sole owners in 1934 and she was finally reported scrapped in the last quarter of 1937.

Vera

Towards the end of 1897 a further steamer was deemed necessary as a spare ship for the LSWR Le Havre and Channel Island services, and this led to the ordering of *Vera* from the Clydebank Engineering and Shipbuilding Company, lately J. & G. Thomson, who had once again come up with the most attractive price and shortest delivery period of 6½-7 months. Launched on 4 July 1898 and delivered in September, at a cost of £54,000, *Vera* had the following main dimensions:

Length: 270ft 0in
Breadth: 35ft 1in
Depth: 14ft 5in
Gross tonnage: 1,193
Machinery: Two sets four-cylinder triple expansion
Boilers: Four SE return tube 200lb/sq in
Power: 4,500ihp
Speed: 19.5kts max (18 in service)

In spite of initiating a return to a single-funnelled profile, this twin-screw steamer was in reality an improved *Columbia*, with slightly increased beam, and a longer superstructure. Other improvements included the substitution of water tube boilers in place of cylindrical ones.

Her career up to the outbreak of World War 1 was without untoward incident, save for a minor collision with the *Simla* in Southampton Water in March 1901. During the war she was credited with shelling and sinking an enemy submarine off the Isle of Wight. After the war she returned to normal service and passed to the Southern Railway in 1923.

In May 1932 the French company which had operated a Jersey to St Malo service since 1919 decided to withdraw and the ageing *Vera* was assigned to reopen the route for the Southern Railway in June of that year. This final brief phase in her career lasted until a new purpose-built steamer, *Brittany*, took over the following year, and *Vera* left Southampton for breaking up by T. W. Ward & Sons on 28 October 1933.

Below: The single-funnelled *Vera* seen here at speed in the Solent served the Channel Islands and French ports well for nearly 35 years. *Author's Collection*

Alberta

Following the tragic loss of *Stella* in 1899, the LSWR quickly approved the construction of a replacement and a contract was signed with their regular builders, who had changed their name yet again to the well-known one of John Brown and Company, Clydebank. Named *Alberta*, she entered service on the Southampton/Channel Islands run in June 1900, and, as can be seen from the following table of particulars, she was very similar in dimension to her predecessor *Vera* though slightly more powerful:

Length: 270ft 0in
Breadth: 35ft 6in
Depth: 14ft 6in
Gross tonnage: 1,240
Machinery: Two sets four-cylinder triple expansion
Boilers: Two DE cylindrical with Serve tubes 200lb/sq in
Power: 5,000ihp
Speed: 19.5kts

She was a good looking ship and marked the end of a long line of Clyde-built reciprocating engined steamers. Her flying bridge was placed in front of her foremast which distinguished her from *Vera* and she also had a different arrangement of boats and ventilators.

She came through World War 1 unscathed, and apart from hitting a rock off Guernsey in July 1920, saw steady and uneventful service throughout the 1920s. With new steamers building, she was withdrawn in December 1929, after having carried nearly three-quarters of a million passengers during her 28½ years in service.

In 1930 she was sold to Inglessi & Son, of Samos, who placed her on the Lesbos/Chios-Piraeus run the following year. Briefly renamed *Mykali* in 1934, she reverted to her original name a year later. At the beginning of World War 2 her owners tried unsuccessfully to sell her to Canada, and she was eventually bombed and sunk at Salamis during the German invasion of Greece in 1941.

Above: Initially *Alberta* had a different bridge arrangement to *Vera* but she could always be identified by her more widely spaced boats and 'forest' of ventilators. *Laurence Dunn Collection*

Right: A later view of *Alberta* in SR colours. Her bridge has been moved back behind the foremast, making it similar to *Vera's* and her promenade deck bulwarks extended.
Author's Collection

Princess Ena

In 1906 the LSWR ended their 10-year association with Clydebank and ordered their next passenger steamer from the East Coast yard of Gourlay Bros Dundee, who had previously completed two 500ton cargo steamers, *Ada* and *Bertha*, for the same company. The new ship was launched at Dundee on 25 May, and was the last of the company's vessels to be given a girl's name, albeit with a royal prefix. *Princess Ena* had the following main particulars:

Length: 250ft 7in
Breadth: 33ft 4in
Depth: 15ft 2in
Gross tonnage: 1,198
Machinery: Two sets three-cylinder triple expansion
Power: 165nhp
Speed: 19kts (contract)

Designed to carry about 600 passengers on the Southampton to St Malo service, she ranked second to *Alberta* in terms of tonnage, but fell far short of that ship in looks. Her short split superstructure and unusually tall funnel gave her a stiff, unbalanced, rather old-fashioned profile, and she was also the last Channel steamer to be built with reciprocating engines.

Notwithstanding these facts, she had a long and useful life, and during World War 1 she was commandeered for ferry service in the Eastern Mediterranean, between Salonika and Mudros. Twice in her career she hit rocks; the Paternosters off Jersey on 19 May 1908, and the Minquiers between Jersey and St Malo on 13 August 1923, but each time she managed to make port and was repaired.

Her luck finally ran out on the afternoon of 3 August 1935, when she caught fire some 10 miles south of Corbiere in Jersey. Abandoned by her passengers and crew, who were picked up by the *St Helier*, she was allowed to burn out and eventually sank some 24hr later. In nearly 30 years of service she had carried almost a million passengers.

Caesarea, Sarnia (1910)

Although slow to adopt the turbine, the LSWR specified this mode of propulsion for two new ships for their Channel Islands service, which were ordered from Messrs Cammell Laird & Co of Birkenhead in 1910. *Caesarea* was the second London and South Western ship to bear the old Roman name for Jersey, whilst *Sarnia*'s name, the equivalent for Guernsey, was new to the Company. Launched on 28 May and 9 July 1910 both ships entered service later that year.

Representing a considerable increase in size over the preceding ships, they had the following main particulars:

Length: 284ft 7in
Breadth: 35ft 2in
Depth: 15ft 8in
Gross tonnage: 1,505/1,498
Machinery: One HP and two LP Parsons turbines driving three shafts

Above: Pictured at speed in Southampton Water the handsome *Caesarea* and her sister *Sarnia* were the only direct-drive triple screw turbine ships in the London & South Western fleet. *Author's Collection*

Right: *Sarnia* with damaged bows after colliding with and sinking the railway cargo ship *Hythe* in October 1915 off Cape Helles near the Dardanelles. *IWM*

Below right: This photograph of the Isle of Man Steam Packet Co's *Manx Maid*, the former *Caesarea*, shows her little altered save for the addition of bulwarks at her bow. *Author's Collection*

Boilers: Two DE Babcock & Wilcox 160lb/sq in
Power: 6,500shp
Speed: 20.5kts

Triple-screw ships, their outward design owed much to *Vera* and *Alberta*, more closely approximating a larger version of the former, with a higher bridge and an extra deck-house and pair of boats aft. Accommodation was provided for 980 passengers in two classes.

Their machinery followed the by now normal pattern of a high-pressure centre turbine, exhausting into two low-pressure wing turbines, each driving a separate screw.

In November 1914, *Sarnia* was commandeered as an armed boarding vessel, being fitted with two 12-pounder guns. Whilst serving in the Mediterranean she collided with and sank the SER cargo steamer *Hythe* off Cape Helles on 28 October 1915, badly damaging her bows. She herself was torpedoed and sunk off Alexandria on 12 September 1918.

Caesarea also acted for a short while in a similar

capacity from November 1914 until December 1915, otherwise continuing on her normal run. On the morning of 7 July 1932 when outward bound from St Helier, she struck the Pignonet Rock off Noirmont Point in dense fog, but whilst endeavouring to return to port she hit the Oyster Rock and, with a leaking stokehold, had to be beached close to the outer breakwater. Raised and towed to Birkenhead for repairs, she was bought by the Isle of Man Steam Packet Company on 27 November to replace their lost *Douglas* (formerly *Dora*).

Converted to oil-firing and renamed *Manx Maid*, she entered Isle of Man to Liverpool service in 1924, continuing thus until the outbreak of war in 1939. Requisitioned as a Fleet Messenger vessel, followed by a spell of trooping, she was renamed HMS *Bruce* in 1941 and from 1942 until 1946 served as a Fleet Air Arm tender. Returned to her owners minus her mainmast, she sailed on summer weekends only until making her last voyage under tow from Douglas to Barrow for scrapping in November 1950. Her career had lasted 40 years, and had spanned two world wars.

Normannia (1912), *Hantonia*

Following the delivery of their first triple screw direct-drive turbine steamers *Caesarea* and *Sarnia* in 1910 the LSWR were quickly in the market again for new tonnage for their Le Havre service. With an eye to economy they stipulated the adoption of twin screw geared turbine machinery for the two ships ordered from the Fairfield Shipbuilding and Engineering Co, Glasgow. They were the first of their type in the world to employ this form of propulsion and were assured of a place in shipping history.

Normannia, the first of the pair, took to the water at Govan on 9 November 1911, followed by her sister on 23 December. The latter was launched as *Louvima* but was renamed *Hantonia* in January. They shared the following main particulars:

Below: The pioneer geared turbine steamer *Normannia* shown in her original colours. She marked a return to twin funnels. *Author's Collection*

Length: 290ft 0in
Breadth: 36ft 0in
Depth: 23ft 6in
Gross tonnage: 1,567
Machinery: Two sets Parsons SR geared turbines
Boilers: One DE and one SE 160lb/sq in
Power: 6,000shp
Speed: 19.5kts (contract)

They were the first twin funnelled steamers built for the railway company since the 1890s-built *Alma* and *Columbia* which they replaced on entering service in 1912. Contrary to fears expressed openly by many, their new machinery had performed faultlessly during trials, showing savings in coal and water consumption when compared with their direct drive counterparts. *Normannia* had reached a maximum speed of 20.4kts on the Skelmorlie mile and 19.7kts during a six hour trial.

Both ships performed steadily and satisfactorily on the Le Havre night service until the outbreak of war in 1939 when sailing frequency was reduced to three per week. *Hantonia* ran between Folkestone and Calais on trooping service that winter before being transferred to the Channel Islands/Brittany ports run and was the last ship to leave St Malo on 16 June 1940 sailing direct to Southampton with 700 passengers. A fortnight previous to this her sister had been sunk by German aircraft six miles west of Mardyck whilst assisting in the evacuation of Dunkirk on 30 May.

Hantonia became a naval accommodation ship in 1942 and was returned to the SR in 1945, resuming her normal run shortly afterwards. She sailed without her mainmast in latter years until replaced by *Normannia* in 1952 when she proceeded to Grays on the River Thames for breaking up by T. W. Ward.

Below: Hantonia **in SR livery in the 1930s. Note the extremely large ventilators.** *Laurence Dunn Collection*

Bottom: Hantonia **at Southampton after the war with her mainmast removed.** *Laurence Dunn Collection*

Lorina

Early in World War 1 the LSWR approached Denny Bros of Dumbarton for the first time, with an order for two new twin-screw turbine passenger ships for the Channel Islands service. Because of the war, however, only one ship was built, being given the name *Lorina*. Taken over by the Admiralty whilst still on the stocks in 1918, she was completed as a troopship and during a six-hour trial in 1919 she reached an average speed of 19.68kts. Released to her owners in 1919, she had the following dimensions:

Length (oa): 299ft 0in
Breadth: 36ft 0in
Depth/Draught: 15ft 9in/13ft 0in
Gross tonnage: 1,457
Machinery: Two sets Parsons SR geared turbines
Boilers: One DE and one SE Scotch 162lb/sq in
Power: 4,830shp (Six hour trial)
Speed: 19.5kts (contract)

She was designed to take the ground at low water, and her profile continued the two-funnelled look introduced by the *Normannia*, though a certain lightness of touch gave her a slight edge in looks over the earlier ship. Her passenger capacity included berths for 148 first class and 90 second class passengers, and her two cargo holds could load 18,650cu ft of freight.

Returned to her owners in 1919, she finally entered her intended service some five years after being ordered. Adopting the SR's black-topped funnels in 1923, she later had solid bulwarks substituted in place of rails at her stern and sometime during the 1930s the white paint was carried down to deck level.

The only untoward incident to mar her career during normal service occurred on 23 September 1935, when she struck a rock near St Helier and suffered considerable hull damage.

Following the outbreak of war in 1939 she was commandeered for troop carrying duties but was dive-bombed and sunk whilst assisting in the evacuation of Dunkirk on 29 May 1940.

Below: A beam view of Lorina *in LSWR colours showing her well balanced profile. Her promenade deck was later enclosed as far as the first stanchion under her second pair of boats.* Author's Collection

Dinard, St Briac

In September 1923 the SR, having absorbed the LSWR, invited tenders for two new ships for the night service to St Malo, and once again Denny Bros who had quoted a price of £255,000 for both ships, were successful in obtaining the order. Built alongside each other, *Dinard* was launched first on 2 May 1924, and her sister *St Briac* exactly a month later. Both averaged about 19.6kts on their trials, and they were delivered on 16 July and 11 September respectively.

Their main particulars were as follows:

Length (oa): 325ft 0in
Breadth: 41ft 0in
Depth/Draught: 15ft 0in/12ft 6in
Gross tonnage: 2,291
(*Dinard* 1,769 as car ferry)
Machinery: Two sets Parsons SR geared turbines
Boilers: One DE and one SE return tube 182lb/sq in coal/oil
Power: 5,300shp
Speed: 19.5kts (contract)

Representing a development of the *Lorina* design, but with plated-in superstructure, they were unusual in having double bottoms, possibly as a safeguard against the ever-present danger of striking rocks in the St Malo

area. Sleeping accommodation was provided for 234 first class passengers in cabins, whilst 118 second class passengers were berthed in saloons and their total daytime complement was around 1,340 persons.

St Briac made several cruises to French Channel ports, including Rouen, during the 1930s, but otherwise both ships ran successfully on the St Malo service until its withdrawal on 6 September 1939 following the outbreak of war. *Dinard* was quickly converted to a hospital ship, and rescued a number of stretcher cases from Dunkirk. Following a period spent at Scapa Flow as a floating hospital for merchant-seamen, she was fitted out for Mediterranean service in 1943, and until her commission ended in March 1944 steamed some 30,000 miles, visiting 30 ports and carrying nearly 7,600 patients. On 7 June

1944, whilst helping to bring back wounded from the Normandy beaches, she hit a mine and was towed back to Southampton for repairs. She returned to transport duties, being refitted in May 1945 to carry troops between Dieppe and Newhaven and between Calais and Dover.

St Briac's war service, on the other hand, had been short, for whilst acting as a Fleet Air Arm target ship, she had been mined and sunk off Aberdeen on 13 March 1942, with the loss of six of her crew.

When finally released, *Dinard* did not return to her prewar service but was sent instead to Palmers yard at Hebburn on Tyne for conversion to a car ferry. This amounted to almost a total rebuild, and she emerged in June 1947 with a new profile and capable of carrying about 70 cars and 360 passengers. She started service on the Dover-Boulogne route on 1 July, but cars had to be craned on and off until stern doors were fitted by the Silley Cox yard at Falmouth in the spring of 1952.

Withdrawn in October 1958, she was sold early the following year to Rederi A/B Vikinglinjen of Mariehamm. Renamed *Viking*, her car capacity was slightly increased during a refit by Aalborg Vaerft, and on 1 June she opened the first roll-on roll-off car ferry service from Mariehamm, being routed to Korpo in Finland and Graddo in Sweden, though the latter was altered to Kapellskar the following year, and the Finnish terminal to Pargas in 1962.

Towards the end of 1965 her ownership was transferred to Rederi A/B Solstad, and the forward end of her boat deck was plated in. In 1967 her Finnish terminal was again changed to Naantali and she adopted the now familiar red livery of Viking Line. She was soon superseded by new purpose-built tonnage, and after making her last trip on 12 August 1970 was laid up, later being towed to Helsinki for scrapping by Helsingin Romulüki who had cut her down to deck level by the spring of 1974.

Ardena

This ship must surely rank as one of the most unusual to serve on the Channel, and is unique in having been converted from a warship. In 1915 the Admiralty had ordered a large class of two-funnelled escort sloops, which were built on merchant ship lines and were designed to replace the hastily converted paddle-steamers which had performed the task up to that time. The new ships were named after plants, being known as the Herbaceous Border class and in all 72 were built in five separate groups.

At the end of the war, some of these ships became surplus to requirements and HMS *Peony*, one of the third group known as the Arabis type, was bought by the London and South Western Railway Company, who were seeking a replacement for their cargo ship *Brittany*, lost during the war. Following reconstruction, she was

Above: This picture of an 'Azalea' class sloop gives an idea of what *Ardena* **looked like when she was HMS** *Peony*. *Laurence Dunn Collection*

Right: *Ardena* **in SR colours showing the complete transformation effected by her conversion. Her hull was not completely flush as it dropped down to a short mooring deck aft. Note also the lack of superstructure.** *P. A. Vicary*

Below right: A rare view of *Ardena* **in Toyias colours in the 1930s. Note how an impression of increased size has been provided by the addition of an extra deck of superstructure and solid bulwarks.** *Laurence Dunn Collection*

renamed *Ardena* and placed on a summer service between Southampton and Cherbourg. Her main particulars were:

Length: 250ft 1in
Breadth: 33ft 1in
Depth: 17ft 4in
Gross tonnage: 1,092
Machinery: Three-cylinder triple expansion by D. Rowan & Co
Power: 2,400shp
Speed: 16kts

Her original builders had been A. Macmillan & Son, Dumbarton and she had been launched on 25 August 1915. As reconstructed, she was basically a dual-purpose ship, carrying both passengers and cargo, and in 1925 she was transferred to the Southampton-Caen service, following the cessation of the cargo service to the French port from Newhaven.

Nothing untoward happened during her new career, indeed, she seems to have been an almost forgotten ship, as very little is written about her, and photographs are hard to come by. The Caen service was discontinued in 1931, and she lay in reserve until July 1934, when she was bought by a Greek company, Navigation Const. Togias, who placed her on the Lesbos to Piraeus service, where she ran in competition with the Inglessi owned *Alberta*. Her owner, EK Togias, later removed and sold off her lead ballast which made her somewhat unstable, though she was credited with the fastest passage on the Lesbos run. She was lost during the war, the exact nature of her demise being unknown.

Isle of Jersey, Isle of Guernsey, Isle of Sark

At the end of 1928 in order to replace *Alberta* and to cope with increasing demand for cheap travel to the Channel Islands, the SR decided to order two new steamers with increased second class accommodation. Dennys were once again chosen as the builders and the first of the pair, *Isle of Jersey*, was launched at Dumbarton on 22 October the following year, closely followed by the *Isle of Guernsey* on 17 December. Both ships were delivered before time, in January and March of 1930, having comfortably reached their contract speed during five and six-hour trials, the figures being 19.67kts and 19.59kts respectively.

Intended for both day and night service, their main dimensions were as follows:

Length: 306ft 0in
Breadth: 42ft 0in
Depth/Draught: 16ft 0in/12ft 6in
Gross tonnage: 2,143

Below: Isle of Jersey passing Calshot inward bound for Southampton after a day crossing from the Channel Islands on 29 September 1947. Laurence Dunn Collection

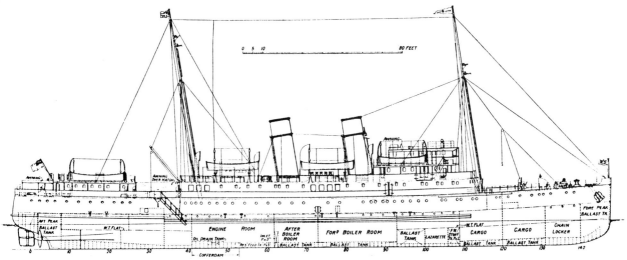

Above left: **Another view of** *Isle of Jersey* **as a wartime hospital ship.** *IWM*

Left: **An aerial photograph of** *Isle of Sark* **showing her curved maierform bow and extended bulwarks forward. Note also the tall ventilators in front of her forward funnel.** *Skyfotos*

Below left: **A rare picture of** *Isle of Jersey* **as the Libyan** *Libda*. **The fact that she is dressed suggests the occasion was her maiden arrival in Tripoli.** *Laurence Dunn Collection*

Machinery: Two sets Parsons SR geared turbines
Boilers: Three SE return tube Scotch 200lb/sq in
Power: 540nhp
Speed: 19.5kts (loaded contract)

Good looking ships, they represented the final evolution of the two-funnelled *Normannia/Hantonia* design and were very similar to *Dinard* and *St Briac*, the main difference being that they had their lifeboats raised and their solid bulwarks were continued right to the stern.

Their success in service was such that the Southern Railway asked for a repeat, accepting Denny's suggestion of a different machinery arrangement. The new ship was named *Isle of Sark* and was delivered at Southampton on 25 January 1932. Apart from her boiler rearrangement she differed externally from the earlier pair in being the first British ship to be fitted with a Maierform bow, and in having extended bow bulwarks. In 1934 she made history by being the first vessel to demonstrate the success of the new Denny-Brown fin stabilisers.

All three sisters continued to run to the Channel Islands until war was declared, when the earlier pair were taken over as hospital ships. *Isle of Jersey* went to Scapa whilst *Isle of Guernsey* took part in the Dunkirk

evacuation, but cumulative damage prevented her from taking any further part after 30 May. Following brief employment as a Fleet Air Arm target ship, she was converted to an Infantry Assault ship in 1943, joining up with her sister again at the Normandy landings. *Isle of Sark* meanwhile had continued on the Channel Islands run up to the 28 June 1940, being tied up in St Peter Port during the air-raid prior to the German occupation. Following a brief spell on Irish Sea service, she became a radar training ship and later an anti-aircraft ship.

All three survived the war, and *Isle of Guernsey* had the distinction of reopening first the Newhaven/Dieppe service, and later the Channel Islands service on 25 June 1945, being joined soon after by her two sisters.

After nearly 15 years regular and satisfactory service, *Isle of Jersey* was the first to be withdrawn at the end of March 1959, being sold a year later to Mohammed Senussi Giabor for pilgrim service under the Libyan flag. After refitting at Smiths Dock on the Tyne, she left for Tripoli as *Libda* on 28 April, and following a rousing welcome on her arrival, was put in hand for further alteration. Work ceased when a foreign company gained the rights to the Libyan pilgrim trade, and she was allowed to deteriorate in a lay-up berth, being eventually sold for scrapping in La Spezia early in 1963.

As the Southampton/Channel Islands service continued to run down, *Isle of Sark* was withdrawn in November 1960. She was sold to the Belgian breakers Van Heyghen Freres for scrap the following March, being towed to Ghent where she arrived on 7 April 1961.

The British Transport Commission continued to operate *Isle of Guernsey* alone on a reduced service, before transferring her to Weymouth following the final closure of the Southampton service on 12 May 1969. Whilst at Weymouth she made several day excursions to Guernsey, including some trips from Torquay. Replaced by the new *Sarnia*, she made her last sailing on 16 June and, after a period spent in reserve, followed her sister to Ghent, where she arrived in tow on 20 November for scrapping.

Brittany (1933)

In October 1932 the SR ordered a new turbine steamer from Wm Denny to replace the elderly *Vera* on their recently revived Channel Islands to France run. Her design was left to the builders, provided railway requirements were met, and this resulted in a handsome and unique looking ship. Launched on 12 April 1933 she was appropriately named *Brittany* and following trials, during which she reached 17.66kts, was handed over at Southampton on 9 June.

She had the following main characteristics:

Length: 260ft 0in
Breadth: 41ft 6in
Depth/Draught: 14ft 0in/10ft 6in
Gross tonnage: 1,522
Machinery: Two sets Parsons single reduction geared turbines
Boilers: One Yarrow w/t and one Scotch cylindrical r/t 250lb/sq in
Power: 2,500shp
Speed: 16kts

Above: *Brittany* had an unmistakable profile which ended the long run of twin funnelled Southampton-based ships. *IA Library*

Right: *Brittany* as the Finnish *Alandsfarjan* after exchanging her yellow hull for the standard red one adopted by Viking Line for all its ships after 1967. Note the extension of her superstructure forward, raised boats and vehicle ramp at her stern. *Viking Line*

A shallow draught steamer she was designed for both day and night service and ran mainly from Jersey and Guernsey to St Malo but also served Alderney, Sark, Cherbourg and Granville on occasions. Due to the large tidal range in this area she was built to take the ground at low water. Her passenger capacity was 850 persons, 500 being in first class, and sleeping berths were provided for 62.

In August 1939 she was making four trips a week between Jersey and St Malo and although war had been declared she continued running thus until the end of December. Following a short stint on leave service between Folkestone and Boulogne she took part in the evacuation of France and in September 1940 was commissioned as an auxiliary netlayer. Refitted at Rosyth early in 1941 she travelled extensively, visiting such places as far apart as Panama, West Africa, Bombay and Columbo. Later she went to the Mediterranean and was present at the invasion of Southern France early in 1944.

Returned to the Southern Railway in 1945 she was refitted and took up her normal peacetime service again in 1947. During the winter months she only ran to St Malo once a week and often returned to Southampton for the rest of the week, sometimes carrying cross-Channel passengers.

She was withdrawn at the end of November 1962 and was laid up in Southampton. In 1963 she was sold to Alandsfarjan A/B of Mariehamn and following alteration to her accommodation in Finland which included the fitting of new public rooms forward and the provision of space for the carriage of 38 cars aft, loading being via a stern ramp, she commenced running between Mariehamn and Graddo, in Sweden, on 20 June 1963. Her new name was *Alandsfarjan* and she sported a yellow hull and funnel, the latter carrying a red band and red shield.

Her Swedish terminal was later changed to Kapellskar and whilst entering the archipelago in fog on 19 May 1972 she grounded off Remmargrund. It was originally intended to tow her to Stockholm but she refloated under her own power, however damage was such that she was declared a constructive total loss. Sold to breakers Wihuri Yhtyma she proceeded to Salo in Finland where demolition started in July.

Falaise

The first cross-Channel steamer to be built for the SR after the war took to the water at Dumbarton on 25 October 1946. Intended primarily for the Southampton to St Malo service, *Falaise* attained a mean speed of 20.97kts during trials on the Skelmorlie mile, and was delivered at Southampton on 14 June 1947. Much larger than *Dinard* and *St Briac*, she had the following main particulars:

Length: 310ft 6in
Breadth: 48ft 0in
Depth/Draught: 17ft 6in/12ft 6in
Gross tonnage: 3,710
Machinery: Two sets Parsons single reduction
               geared turbines
Boilers: Two Foster Wheeler w/t 450lb/sq in

Power: 8,500shp
Speed: 20.5kts

In appearance she followed the new styling introduced by *Invicta* but her upper deck was continued to the stern, and she had fewer windows in her superstructure, being intended mainly for night service. Her original passenger complement was for 1,527 persons carried in two classes, including 338 sleeping berths, and for passenger comfort she was fitted with stabilisers.

Below: *Falaise* **makes a fine picture on her official speed trials, looking every bit a 'liner in miniature'.**
Laurence Dunn Collection

Top: Looking very different immediately after her conversion to a car ferry, with bridge cabs removed and new ventilators. Her hull colour was changed to dark blue towards the mid-'60s and the paint line was carried up to deck level forward of her bridge front. At the same time the black top to her funnel was narrowed for about a year and soon afterwards the Joint Service Flag was added.
Newhaven and Seaford Historical Society

Above: *Falaise* in Sealink colours off Jersey in June 1973 near the end of her career. Note her large stern door. *Author*

She spent 16 years on the St Malo run but during that time saw service on several other routes, notably relieving *Normannia* on the Southampton-Le Havre service during the latter's overhaul and also on the Channel Islands run and the Golden Arrow service in the winter of 1947-48. She also undertook cruises each year in late spring to early summer, carrying 216 passengers to French ports, including Rouen, and the Channel Islands. Additionally, in May 1961 she made two cruises to Holland and Belgium from Folkestone to view the spring bulbs.

At the end of the 1963 season the decision was taken to convert her to a stern-loading car ferry for a proposed new roll-on, roll-off service between Newhaven and Dieppe, which was scheduled to start in 1964. The work was undertaken by the Palmer Hebburn yard of Vickers Armstrongs and she inaugurated the new service on 1 June, her new capacity being 100 cars of which 75 could be carried on the main deck and a further 25 on an upper deck reached by a folding ramp. Her gross tonnage was reduced to 2,416 and she could now carry 700 passengers in one class.

Following the entry into service of SNCF's two new car ferries in the summer of 1965 *Falaise* was relegated to off-peak sailings and after the completion of British Rail's new *Senlac* in the spring of 1973 she was transferred to Weymouth, her livery being changed from the special Newhaven Joint Service one to that of Sealink. At the beginning of June she opened the first ro-ro car ferry service to Jersey which was so successful that it was continued throughout the winter on a twice weekly basis. In June 1974 she made the first scheduled car ferry sailing from Guernsey, using St Peter Port's new linkspan.

The 1974 summer season was intended to be her last but engine trouble occurring early in August became so severe that she had to be withdrawn on the 14th of that month and was taken to Holyhead for survey, being replaced four days later by the chartered Scandinavian ferry *Svea Drott*. Her condition was found to be so poor that she was sold to Spanish breakers in Bilbao and she arrived there in tow of the German tug *Fairplay XII* on the last day of 1974.

Normannia (1952)

Discussions on the design of a new passenger ship to replace *Hantonia* on the Southampton-Le Havre overnight service first got under way between the British Transport Commission and Denny Bros in 1948. The resulting ship was named *Normannia* at her launch on 19 July 1951 and after reaching a mean speed of 20.62kts on the measured mile was handed over to her owners for management by their Southern Region during the following January. Dimensionally she was very similar to *Falaise* as can be seen from the following table of her particulars:

Length: 308ft 11in
Breadth: 48ft 0in
Depth/Draught: 17ft 6in/12ft 6.5in
Gross tonnage: 3,543
Machinery: Two sets Pametrada double reduction geared turbines
Boilers: Two Foster Wheeler w/t 350lb/sq in
Power: c8000shp
Speed: 19.5kts (loaded contract)

She differed externally from *Falaise* in having a flush hull and a more compact superstructure which was topped by two tripod masts and a rather ugly funnel with a sloping top that did not match the paint-line between black and buff. She was one of the first Channel steamers to be fitted with Pametrada turbines and her complement of about 1,400 passengers in two classes included berthing accommodation for 325 persons.

Although confined to the year-round Le Havre run for most of her earlier life she made occasional relief voyages on other routes such as Harwich to the Hook in the autumn of 1953, following a visit to the Coronation Naval Review the previous June. In November 1958 in addition to her normal duties, she instigated occasional winter visits to the Channel Islands and sometimes St Malo, operating out of Weymouth for short periods early in 1960 and again in March 1963. In May 1960 she made two weekend cruises from Dover to Antwerp and Ostend, and Amsterdam.

Following her last sailing from Le Havre on 3 December 1963 shortly before the route was closed she was sent to Hawthorn Leslie Ltd at Hebburn-on-Tyne for a £280,000 conversion to a stern loading car ferry. Her accommodation was stripped and her main and upper decks altered to carry 111 cars whilst her passenger capacity was reduced to 500. With her gross tonnage reduced to 2,217 she made her inaugural car ferry voyage

Below: Reviving the name of the pioneer geared-turbine ship, Normannia did not fit into any recognisable pattern when compared with other Denny-built ships.
Laurence Dunn Collection

between Dover and Boulogne on 21 April. Although this was to be her usual route she sailed out of Newhaven on several occasions and on 9 July 1965 inaugurated a new Irish Sea car ferry service between Holyhead and Dun Laoghaire in place of the *Holyhead Ferry 1* whose construction had been delayed.

In April 1973 she was transferred for six months to the SNCF for Calais-Dover service and from December to the following March replaced *Falaise* on the new Channel Island car ferry service from Weymouth.

On 1 July 1974 she struck an underwater obstruction in Dover harbour whilst shifting berth and flooded her engine-room and car deck. After repairs lasting three months she returned in October to the Channel Islands run for a further nine months. In July of 1976 she opened yet another new service, this time between Dover and Dunkirk West, following which she was put on the sale list. However breakdowns on other routes kept her fairly busy as a reserve ship until finally laid up at Newhaven in May 1978.

Her reported sale to Red Sea Ferries of Dubai for pilgrim use under Panamanian flag fell through, but not before a thin white line had been added to her funnel. After several false starts she finally left for scrapping in Spain on 29 November 1978 and after calling at Falmouth and Brest en route arrived at Gijon early on 6 December to await the attentions of Desguaces Heme S.A.

Below: *Normannia* **after her 1964 conversion to a car ferry showing the extensions at both ends of her superstructure. This picture was taken in June 1973 whilst she was on charter to SNCF.** *Author*

Bottom: **Pictured at Newhaven on 14 November 1978 following her abortive sale for Red Sea pilgrim use. Her damaged bow led to delays in obtaining a seaworthiness certificate for her final voyage to Spanish shipbreakers a fortnight later.** *Author*

PART 6
Weymouth to Channel Islands/St Malo

1889–1947 GWR
1/1948–11/1948 British Transport Commission (Western Region)
11/1948–1962 British Transport Commission (Southern Region)*
1963–1978 British Rail Board
1979–to date Sealink UK
*St Patrick remained under Western Region management until 17th December 1959
Note Both St Patrick's (1930 and 1948) were registered in the name of the
Fishguard & Rosslare Railways and Harbours Co

Lynx, Antelope, Gazelle

In 1871 the GWR had obtained by Parliamentary process the requisite powers to operate their own steamers, but it was not until August 1889 that they decided to run the Weymouth-Channel Islands service themselves. To suit their purpose they took over the Weymouth and Channel Islands Steam Packet Company's ships, at the same time ordering three new twin-screw steamers from Laird Brothers, the well-known Birkenhead shipyard. The first purpose-built ships for the service, they represented a considerable advance on the previous paddle-steamers.

All three ships were delivered in the late summer of 1889, their names being *Lynx*, *Antelope* and *Gazelle*, and their main particulars were:

Length: 235ft 6in
Breadth: 27ft 7in
Depth: 13ft 1in
Gross tonnage: 596
Machinery: Two sets triple expansion
Boilers: Two SE 150lb/sq in
Power: 1,700ihp
Speed: 16kts

Their design was left to the shipyard, provided they met the railway company's requirements particularly in relation to draught, Weymouth at that time being very shallow, and they were given long shallow hulls, topped with a turtle-deck foc'sle, and a long bride deck. Two tall raking masts contrasted with two closely placed, rather insignificant funnels to give them an unmistakable but rather discordant profile. However their machinery, specified by Lairds, was of the triple expansion type and was the first twin-screw installation to be used in Channel service. The two propellers overlapped slightly, the starboard one being a little ahead of the port one, bronze ones being used for the summer service, and iron ones during the winter.

Their original passenger certificate was for 431 persons, but after only a year in service a new ladies' cabin was placed aft of the bridge, necessitating the

Left: *Antelope* entering Weymouth during her first year of service. Shortly afterwards her forward boats and funnels were raised following the addition of a new saloon. Note the small sail on the foremast.
Author's Collection

Above right: *Lynx* during her wartime service as the minesweeper *Lynn.* Note that her taller funnels have sloping tops. *IWM*

Right: *Gazelle* after her conversion to a cargo ship in 1908 had a new hatch and kingpost between her bridge and funnels. *Author's Collection*

Below: A fine quarter view of *Gazelle* coming astern into Weymouth. Compare the different boat arrangement with the view of *Antelope.* *Author's Collection*

raising of the first pair of lifeboats and the lengthening of the funnels.

Superseded by newer tonnage, *Gazelle* was converted to a cargo ship early in 1908, and her sister *Lynx* in 1912 following a spell on the Plymouth-Nantes run. *Antelope* ran for a while in 1910 from Plymouth to Brest and was sold in August 1913 for only £4,500 to S.A. Ionienne de Nav a Vapew, a Pyraeus-based firm owned by Yannoulatos, who renamed her *Atromitos*.

During World War 1 *Gazelle* and *Lynx* (renamed *Lynn* to avoid confusion with a destroyer of the same name) were used as minesweepers by the Admiralty from 27 October 1914. Shortly afterwards *Lynn* had the

coincidence of arresting her former sister *Atromitos* for running contraband in the Mediterranean. *Gazelle* became a minelayer for six months from May 1915 based at Mudros. Released in March and April 1920 respectively, they continued somewhat intermittently as cargo carriers until sold for scrap in 1925.

Atromitos soldiered on in the Mediterranean passing in 1929 to the ownership of Hellenic Coast Lines, and was eventually sold to Italy for scrap in 1933. A true pioneer as far as the GWR's Weymouth service was concerned, she had lasted well for 44 years, a tribute to the expertise of her builders.

Ibex

The GWR returned to Lairds with an order for a larger steamer to match the rival LSWR's *Frederica* class. Named *Ibex*, the new ship made her first crossing in September 1891 and soon beat the *Lydia*'s record. Primarily an enlarged version of the earlier ships, her main characteristics were as follows:

Length: 265ft 0in
Breadth: 32ft 6in
Depth/Draught: 14ft 2in/11ft 1in
Gross tonnage: 1,160
Machinery: Two sets triple expansion
Boilers: Two DE Scotch 160lb/sq in
Power: 4,000ihp
Speed: 19kts

Her steel hull was divided into ten watertight compartments and she had a long combined bridge and foc'sle, separated from the poop by a short well aft of the

main mast. She was given two taller and more substantial funnels, though these were still closely spaced. Her accommodation included 210 berths, and her maximum passenger capacity was 600.

In 1897 she struck the Noirmontaise Rock off Jersey whilst engaged in a race with *Frederica* and was holed, later being towed to St Helier by *Reindeer*. She did not get off so lightly when on 5 January 1900 she again hit a rock, this time one of the Platte Fougeres off Guernsey, and 15min later settled on the bottom on an even keel some three miles north of St Peter Port, two of her crew having been lost. Following protracted salvage

Below: *Ibex* was rather a stiff looking ship but she proved more than a match in speed for the rival LSWR's 'Frederica' class. This view of her leaving Weymouth shows clearly her well deck aft and the pair of boats added to her poop in 1910, when her funnel cowls were also removed.
Author's Collection

operations by a Hamburg-based company, she was refloated on 21 July and later taken to Birkenhead for a complete refit. Her promenade deck was extended aft, bridging over the short well and she returned to Weymouth in April the following year virtually a new ship.

Around 1910 a third pair of boats were added to her poop, and she remained on the Channel Islands run throughout World War 1, during the course of which she collided with and sank the GWR cargo ship *Aletta* off Weymouth in 1917. She continued on postwar service until her withdrawal in November 1925, and was sold the following year to breakers at Sharpness. Accidents apart, she had led a useful life of 34 years.

Roebuck, Reindeer

In 1896, with cross-Channel competition between the SWR and the GWR at its height, the latter company ordered a pair of larger and faster steamers for a new daytime express service, eschewing Lairds in favour of the Naval Construction and Armaments Company of Barrow (later Vickers-Armstrongs). The new ships closely followed the lines of *Ibex*, the only noticeable difference being that their hulls appeared completely flush with shell doors covering small wells aft. *Roebuck*, the first of the two, was launched on 6 March 1897. On her maiden crossing on 1 July she reached Guernsey in the record time of just under 3½hr, her consort on the daylight service being *Ibex* until the arrival of her sister *Reindeer* early in August.

The main particulars of both ships were:

Length: 280ft 0in
Breadth: 34ft 6in
Depth: 16ft 8in
Gross tonnage: 1,281
Machinery: Two sets triple expansion
Boilers: Two DE 175lb/sq in
Power: 5,300ihp
Speed: 20kts

On 26 January 1905 *Roebuck* caught fire at Milford and sank from the weight of water pumped into her. Refloated nine days later she spent several months repairing at Barrow. The same vessel met with a more serious accident on the morning of 19 July 1911, when she struck the Kaines Rocks near St Brelades, shortly after leaving St Helier. Striking at high water, in an area where the tidal range is amongst the greatest in the world, she was literally and spectacularly left 'high and dry' at low tide with her bows pointing skywards. Towed off nine days later by one of Svitzer's salvage vessels, she eventually underwent three months' repair by Harland and Wolff at Southampton.

Following the outbreak of war in 1914, *Reindeer* was transferred to the Fishguard-Rosslare service for about three weeks, until she was requisitioned along with her sister in October. Fitted out as auxiliary minesweepers, *Roebuck* was lost at Scapa on 13 January 1915 after dragging her anchors and impaling herself on the ram bow of HMS *Imperieuse*.

Reindeer proceeded to the Mediterranean where she took part in the Gallipoli campaign. On release in 1919, she was refitted at Southampton and returned to service in February 1920. Replaced by two new steamers in 1925, she was held in reserve for a while, being used on day excursions to Guernsey the following summer. With her survey overdue she was finally withdrawn in February 1928 and was sold for scrapping in November to T. W. Ward of Briton Ferry.

Below: Roebuck seen here at Weymouth and her sister had a more exaggerated rake to their masts and funnels than the previous steamer, also an extra pair of boats aft. Note the shell doors in the open position. Author's Collection

Left: An unusual picture of *Roebuck* showing her ornately elegant stern. *Author's Collection*

Below: *Reindeer* during her wartime commission as a minesweeper in the northern Aegean. Note the false bow wave and absence of cowls on her funnels. *IWM*

Above: After the war *Reindeer's* **funnels were found to be so damaged that they had to be replaced with new ones, which had sloping tops.** *Author's Collection*

St Julien, St Helier

In the mid-1920s, with the youngest of their ships being some 27 years old, the GWR were faced with the task of renewing their cross-Channel fleet and an order was duly placed for a pair of new turbine steamers with the well known shipbuilders John Brown & Company. The first to be completed, *St Julien*, arrived at Weymouth on 4 May 1925, and made her maiden voyage on a night-sailing to the Channel Islands on the 24th. Her sister *St Helier*, having been launched at Clydebank on 26 March, was delivered on 7 June and from the 29th of that month both ships started a new accelerated summer day service.

Their main dimensions were:

Length: 291ft 3in
Breadth: 42ft 6in
Depth/Draught: 16ft 4in/13ft 1.25in
Gross tonnage: 1,885
Machinery: Two sets Parsons SR geared turbines
Boilers: Four SE oil-fired 230lb/sq in
Power: 4,350shp
Speed: 18kts service (19.5kts trials)

They were given two funnels, the after one being a dummy, and their hulls had a short foc'sle and a significant docking bridge at the stern. Their passenger certificate was for a total of 1,004 passengers, carried in two classes, and berths were provided for 140.

Early in 1928 both ships were given a new profile by the removal of their dummy funnel to lessen windage, and by the deletion of their aft docking bridge. Their appearance was further altered during a 1937 refit when their funnels were reduced in height by 5ft and fitted with a naval type cowl. At the same time internal alterations

resulted in the elimination of the distinctive shelter windows at the forward end of the promenade deck, gross tonnage being slightly increased as a result.

When war was declared in 1939 *St Julien* was quickly taken up as a hospital ship and both sisters took part in the evacuation of troops and refugees from Dunkirk, *St Helier* lifting over 10,000 people in the course of four trips. After visiting other Channel ports, *St Helier* left La Pallice for Plymouth in June, and was sent to Liverpool for repairs. Following a brief spell carrying prisoners of war from Gourock to the Isle of Man, she was requisitioned by the Navy in November and was used for a while as a depot ship for coastal forces at Dartmouth. In June 1942, work started on her conversion to an infantry assault ship, carrying six landing craft and 180 troops. Based at Southampton, she took part in the Normandy landings, united once again with her sister, which had spent 10 months of the previous year in the Mediterranean, having been present at the Anzio landings. On D-Day plus one *St Julien* hit a mine but managed to return to harbour.

After release in 1945, both ships were refitted and took up station at Weymouth again in 1946. Following the Nationalisation of the railway companies in 1948, they were transferred to the management of the Southern Region of the British Transport Commission on 1 November, and were given white painted foc'sle and bulwarks. This phase lasted until 1959 when the level of black hull paint was raised to the top of the bulwarks.

With their replacements ordered from Samuel White in Cowes, in November 1957, they were living on borrowed time, and following the withdrawal of the Paddington 'Boat Trains' in September 1959, both ships

Top: *St Helier* as built with two tall funnels, the after one a dummy which was later removed. Her prominent docking bridge can be seen on the after deckhouse. *Author's Collection*

Above: *St Julien* after her 1937 refit with shortened funnel and cowl top. Note also the alterations to the forward part of her superstructure. *Author's Collection*

Left: *St Julien* as a hospital ship at Newhaven early in World War 2. Her funnel cowl has been removed. *IWM*

were laid up for the winter. After a final summer season they were withdrawn within a fortnight of each other in September 1966, and were laid up awaiting disposal. Having been together for nearly all their 35 years they were not to be separated in their demise, and both were towed to Belgium for scrapping, *St Helier* leaving Weymouth in December for Antwerp and the attentions of Jos de Smedt, whilst *St Julien* went to Van Heyghen Freres at Ghent the following April. Stripped of her fittings, she is reported to have lain for a while at Walcheren as a rest and recreation centre for dockers.

Below: *St Helier* pictured without her landing craft following her conversion to an infantry landing ship in 1942. *IWM*

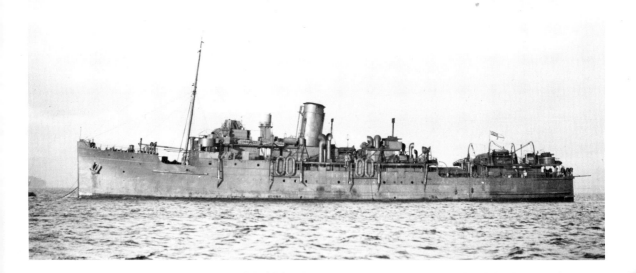

Right: *St Helier* in Southern Region colours at Weymouth in the summer of 1957. Note the extra large davits which were fitted during reconstruction after the war, her own having been lost. Her black hull paint was carried one strake higher after 1959. *Author*

St Patrick (1930)

To replace a namesake which had burned out in April 1929, and the ageing *Reindeer*, a new *St Patrick* was ordered from Alexander Stephens and was launched at their Linthouse Yard on 15 January 1930. Although registered in the ownership of the Fishguard and Rosslare Railways and Harbours Company, she was designed to operate on both the Fishguard and Weymouth services. A little larger than the John Brown built pair, she had the following particulars:

Length: 281ft 4in
Breadth: 41ft 1in

Above: *St Patrick* was a single funnelled version of the earlier 'Saints' with her superstructure extended forward to the break of her foc'sle and solid bulwarks around her stern. She is pictured here at the 1937 review of the fleet by HM King George VI. *Laurence Dunn Collection*

Depth/Draught: 16ft 4in/13ft 3in
Gross tonnage: 1,922
Machinery: Two sets Parsons SR geared turbines by builders
Boilers: Four Babcock & Wilcox oil-fired w/t 230lb/sq in
Power: 4,720shp
Speed: 19kts

Externally the main difference between her and her predecessors was the merging of the foc'sle into her superstructure. Internally she had 11 watertight bulkheads instead of 10, and diesel generators were used in her engine-room.

She made her first sailing from Weymouth on 18 April 1930, following a three-week delay occasioned by the repair of rudder damage incurred during her first berthing at the Dorset port. Just over two years later, whilst approaching Jersey in foggy weather on 5 August,

she struck the Frouquie Rock near Corbiere and flooded her boiler-room. Disabled, she was towed to St Helier the following day by *St Julien* and *Princess Ena*. Repairs were later effected at Birkenhead.

Following the outbreak of war she was employed as a trooper for a while in October 1939 but returned to her normal Irish Sea service between Fishguard and Rosslare. Whilst approaching the Welsh port on Friday, 13 June 1941 she was dive-bombed and sank after breaking in half with the loss of 30 lives, including that of her master.

St Patrick (1948)

Having lost two of their ships, *St David* and *Patrick*, during the war the GWR was quick to seek replacements and in 1946 placed an order with Messrs Cammell Laird & Co, Birkenhead for two new sister ships. They were given similar names to the war losses but although these suggested Irish Sea use *St Patrick* was also intended to

run regularly between Weymouth and the Channel Islands during the summer months.

St David was launched on 6 February 1947 and her sister first took to the water on 20 May following her naming by Lady Portal, wife of the GWR chairman. Upon completion in September the former made a brief

117

visit to Weymouth and the Islands in order to gain berthing experience. *St Patrick* was not delivered until 23 January by which time the GWR had been absorbed into the British Transport Commission however being officially registered in the name of the Fishguard & Rosslare Railways & Harbours Co she was unaffected and retained her original GWR livery of red funnel with a black top.

Her main particulars were as follows:

Length (oa): 321ft 4in
Breadth: 48ft 0in
Depth/Draught: 17ft 2in/13ft 3in
Gross tonnage: 3,482
Machinery: Two sets Parsons single reduction geared turbines
Boilers: Three Babcock & Wilcox oil-fired w/t 250lb/sq in
Power: 8,500shp
Speed: 20kts

She was a handsome steamer with her single funnel and two masts of unequal height and her superstructure was a deck higher than on previous Weymouth ships. She could accommodate some 1,300 passengers in two classes and berths were provided for 295 of these, whilst about 50 cars could be carried in her holds.

She made her first visit to the Channel Islands on 4 February 1948 and for the next 16 summers ran regularly to the Islands from Weymouth with occasional excursions from Torquay. Her winters were mainly spent laid up as a reserve ship in Holyhead harbour and in 1950 and 1951 she ran for a time between that port and Dun Laoghaire. On 17 September 1950 she sustained bottom damage after grounding in St Helier harbour in a gale

and had to proceed to Penarth for repairs. The remainder of the 1950s passed without undue incident and on 17 December 1959 she was permanently transferred to Weymouth under the ownership of the Southern Region of the BTC whose colours she adopted during her spring refit.

In 1961 she underwent a major refit to alter her accommodation to one class and thus bring her into line with the two new Weymouth ships. The work was undertaken by the Mountstuart Dry Dock Co at Cardiff and her gross tonnage was reduced slightly to 3,459 whilst at the same time her black hull paint was raised about 4ft. Lack of space precluded the proposed fitting of stabilisers.

St Patrick ended her regular service at Weymouth on 10 October 1963 and was transferred to Southampton to replace *Normannia* on the Le Havre service. On the first day of the following February she damaged her bows after hitting the outer dock wall at Southampton and had to undergo two weeks of repair at Cardiff. This loss-making service was finally wound up after her 10 May departure from Le Havre and the next day she replaced *Falaise* on the summer St Malo service with additionally a fortnightly trip from that port to Weymouth to allow a day trip. She made a final sailing to Weymouth on 23 September and closed the Southampton-St Malo link for good four days later, thus ending her regular service on the Western Channel.

Early in October she was one of the first BTC ships to be repainted in their new livery and at the same time her hull paint reverted to its original depth and the black top to her funnel was narrowed by some three feet to make space for the new BR logo. Following a six-week refit at Smith's Dock, West Hartlepool during which she was fitted with four shell doors for gangways on either side of her superstructure she left on 15 December to take up a new career on the Dover Strait.

Initially she ran from Dover and Folkestone to Calais but on 29 May 1965 she took up the *Canterbury*'s old seasonal Folkestone-Boulogne service on which she continued for the next six years. During this period she returned to the Channel Islands and St Malo on a number of occasions or as a relief ship on specials, the last occasion being for a week in May 1971.

With plans for the conversion of Folkestone to roll-on, roll-off operation and new multi-purpose ships under construction in France, 1971 was *St Patrick*'s last season and on 29 September she proceeded to Newhaven for lay up. She was sold the following year to Gerasimos S. Fetouris of Piraeus who renamed her *Thermopylae* and placed her on a service linking Italy and Greece. This was not a success and she changed hands locally in 1973 her new owners being Agapitos Bros who renamed her *Agapitos 1* and ran her for the next two years between Piraeus and the Cyklades Islands of Syros, Tenos and Mykonos. Replaced by *Apollon* (ex *Lisieux*) she was laid up at Perama where she has remained rusting ever since and it now seems highly unlikely that the once proud 'Paddy', the last GWR link with the English Channel, will ever put to sea again.

Top left: *St Patrick* leaving Weymouth towards the end of her 1957 season on the Channel Islands service. She is still in the old Great Western colours. *Author*

Centre left: *St Patrick* arriving at St Helier in BR colours on a weekend excursion in September 1970. *Author*

Left: Pictured at Piraeus in her final guise as Agapitos Bros *Agapitos I*. Note the new shell door in her hull and altered superstructure aft. *Author's Collection*

Caesarea, Sarnia (1960)

Breaking new ground in that they were ordered from the Cowes yard of J. Samuel White & Co Ltd these two turbine steamers were intended to replace the ageing *St Julien* and *St Helier* on the Weymouth-Channel Islands run. Their construction marked an act of faith on the part of the Southern Region of the British Transport Commission as the route had been a loss maker for a number of years.

Caesarea was launched on 29 January 1960 followed by *Sarnia* on 6 September, their names resurrecting those used by the LSWR for its first turbine steamers back in 1912. Designed for both day and night crossings they entered service on 2 December 1960 and 17 June 1961 respectively and their main particulars were:

Length (oa): 322ft 0in
Breadth: 51ft 2in
Depth/Draught: 16ft 6in/13ft 7in
Gross tonnage: 4,174
Machinery: Two sets double reduction Pametrada turbines
Boilers: Two Foster Wheeler w/t 360lb/sq in
Power: 9,000shp (max.)
Speed: 20kts (service)

Five deck ships with a tall, compact superstructure they could accommodate 1,400 passengers in one class, sleeping berths being provided for 110 in de luxe (4), single (12) and double cabins (50) with the remainder in a sleeping lounge. Aircraft type seats were also provided, an additional 146 being fitted during annual overhaul in 1971. Equipment included bow rudder and stabilisers.

Thanks to the improved amenities of both ships passenger figures again began to rise during the 1960s, showing a spectacular increase following the electrification of the Waterloo to Bournemouth line in

Below: Caesarea on initial trials in the Solent showing her basic similarity to Normannia. This illusion was destroyed when her black hull paint was raised one deck higher before her entry into service. Beken of Cowes

Right: Sarnia leaving Weymouth in 1966 wearing the new BR livery of monastral blue hull, red funnel with white logo and grey masts. Author

Below right: Sarnia as Aquamart lying in the West India Dock following her abortive 'duty free shopping' service between Ostend and Dunkirk. Her hull was dark red, upperworks and funnel stone-coloured and the design on the latter was in red white and blue. Author

the summer of 1967. The only appreciable amount of time spent away from the Channel Islands run during their first 15 years was when *Sarnia* stood in for *Invicta* on the 'Golden Arrow' service from Dover between 19 November 1962 and 30 January 1963, *Caesarea* doing likewise from December 1966 to January 1967.

Following the opening of a new roll-on, roll-off service to Jersey by *Falaise* in June 1973 and the subsequent purchase by British Rail of the Swedish car ferry *Svea Drott*, one of the two passenger ships became surplus to requirements and *Caesarea* was withdrawn following her last crossing on 6 October. Transferred to Dover she spent the summer of 1976 running between there and Calais and the following year ran between Folkestone and Boulogne.

In the meantime plans to replace *Sarnia*, by now operating in summer only, with a roll-on, roll-off ship in 1977 fell through and she continued until 10 September when she was laid up at Weymouth and put on the sale list for a price of only £80,000. The following May she was purchased by Channel Cruise Lines Ltd, a new company based in Guernsey, and left for drydocking at Immingham on the 24th. Refitted at Grimsby and renamed *Aquamart* she opened a new excursion service on 24 July between Ostend and Dunkirk offering duty free shopping on board. The proposed itinerary was four trips a day carrying up to 800 passengers paying £5 a

head, however strong objections were raised by the Belgian revenue authorities and the service had to be wound up after only a few days. *Aquamart* was taken to London's West India dock on 4 August 1977 where she was de-stored and laid up. Some five months later she found buyers in Greece and was towed away to Piraeus by the Dutch tug *Groenland* on 20 January 1979. Her name had been changed to *Golden Star* and her former name and funnel markings had been painted out. At present she lies off Piraeus and presumably her new owners, Grecian Fertility Inc, intend to convert her for cruising in Greek waters.

Meanwhile *Caesarea* had continued on her seasonal Dover-Calais service during 1978 and 1979, being laid up in Calais during the winter months. On the last day of January 1979 she had made an unusual visit to the Thames for drydocking at Millwall, just missing her former sister.

By now the sole surviving British example of a traditional English Channel passenger ferry, *Caesarea* completed her last season on the short sea route on 27th September 1980, having operated mainly between Folkestone and Boulogne. In view of her historic interest however she made an extra week of special excursions from Dover to Boulogne, undertaking her final crossing from Folkestone on 4 October with a charter in aid of the RNLI.

Although she had been on the sale list for some time no buyer had been forthcoming and she proceeded to Newhaven for lay up on the 8th. *Caesarea* was sold to Superluck Enteprises SA on 8 December 1980 and sailed for Hong Kong nine days later as the Panamanian *Aesarea*. Her departure brings to a close yet another chapter in the annals of British shipping history.

Below: *Caesarea* **passes into history as the last British flag example of a traditional cross-Channel passenger steamer.** *Author*

Bibliography

Books

Boat Trains and Channel Packets, Rixon Bucknall
British Nationalised Shipping, Clegg and Styring
The Centenary of the Ostend-Dover Line
Cross Channel & Coastal Paddle Steamers, Frank Burtt
The Denny List, David John Lyon
English Channel Packet Boats, Grasemann and McLachlan
The Great Western at Weymouth, J. H. Lucking
A History of the Southern Railway, C. F. Dendy Marshall
Lloyd's Register of Shipping
Mailships of the Channel Islands, Richard Mayne
Newhaven-Dieppe, Peter S. Bailey
Newhaven-Dieppe 1825-1980, B. M. E. O'Mahoney
Railway and other Steamers, Duckworth & Langmuir

Periodicals

Engineering, The Engineer, Fairplay, Marine News, Motor Ship, Sea Breezes, The Shipbuilder, Shipbuilding & Shipping Record, Shipping World, Syren & Shipping, Ships Illustrated, Ships Monthly

Right: A wartime view of *Invicta* and *Canterbury* during Channel manoeuvres in preparation for the 1944 invasion of Normandy. Along with other well known Channel steamers they were part of the Force J Assault Group. *IWM*

Below: The Southern Railway's elegant turbine steamer *Engadine* pulls away from Folkestone quay on a December day in 1928. *Author's Collection*

Index